Fare
Kent

Assisted emigration from Kent in the nineteenth century

Helen Allinson

SYNJON BOOKS

2008

ISBN 978 0904373 13 4

Published by Synjon Books 2008

Synjon Books
5 Homestead View
The Street, BORDEN
Sittingbourne, Kent
ME9 8JQ
United Kingdom

CONTENTS

3

For my parents, who founded Synjon Books.

Foreword

This book has two parts which tell separate, yet related stories of how thousands of poor people from Kent set out to find better lives on the other side of the world. The first part looks at the period roughly from 1820-1850 when parishes, acting alone, and then through the poor law unions paid the money necessary to send the poor on their way to the other side of the world. The second part looks at how the Kent Agricultural Labourers Union helped Kentish farm workers and their families to emigrate to New Zealand during the 1870s.

Acknowledgements

I am grateful to Professor Robards of Australia who generously shared with me all his research on his Robard ancestors from Sandhurst, and to Daphne Guthrie who provided me with information about her Mexted ancestors. Thanks are due to Brian Winter the archivist of Whitby, Canada who was able to demonstrate that Stockbury emigrants had settled there. Thanks too, to the staff of the Centre for Kentish Studies for their efficient help. The illustrations from the early editions of the Illustrated London News, are reproduced with permission from the volumes in the Templeman Library of the University of Kent. Andy Straw has kindly allowed me to use the photographs of his ancestors John and Ellen Stroud.

As always my parents John and Dorothea Teague, encouraged me to write the book. My brother Tony Teague has put a lot of time and effort into getting the book ready for the printers. Most of all my thanks to my husband Barry for his thorough editing of the text.

Abbreviations used in footnotes:

CKS	Centre for Kentish Studies
NA	National Archives
CCA	Canterbury Cathedral Archives
Arch Cant	Archaeologia Cantiana

Introduction

During the first half of the 19th century rapid expansion of the population of England caused widespread unemployment and poverty. Between 1801 and 1831 the population of Britain soared from 10 million to 16 million and large numbers of people were without work. The end of the Napoleonic Wars in 1815 also increased unemployment dramatically as thousands of men discharged from the navy, army and transport services looked for employment. Men were laid off from industries that had flourished during the war. In rural areas wages were falling whilst the price of bread remained high.

In the south east of England improved systems of farming meant less work for the farm labourers. Poor rates rose steeply, causing (in some areas) an enormous financial burden to fall on the ratepayers. The system of helping the poor, unchanged since the 16th century, was no longer adequate and some members of the government saw emigration as a way of bringing the poor rates down. The first papers on state assisted emigration were written in 1817, and by 1819 the Poor Law Committee was speaking of encouraging emigration.[1] Wilmot-Horton Under-Secretary of State for the Colonies between 1822 and 1828 was a strong supporter of the idea of state-aided emigration to remove the surplus population of poor people. A great deal of public attention was drawn to the issue by the reports of

---

[1] Johnston H, British emigration policy 1815-30, (1972)

Horton's Select Committees on emigration in 1826 and 1827.

Obviously the poor could not afford to pay their own fares, even though to get to America or Canada in the 1820s could cost less than £5. Australia was out of the question since it cost as much as £40 steerage. So in order for the poor to leave Britain, some method of helping them on their way would have to be devised.

Rural unrest in the south of England in 1830-31 brought more government discussion about the need for assisted emigration and in 1831 a commission was created to look at enabling assisted emigration to the colonies. This culminated in the Poor Law Act of 1834.

It was thought that emigration could be doubly useful to Britain, for not only could the numbers of the poor be reduced here, but also those very same emigrants might prosper in the colonies and become customers for goods made in Britain.

Of course Kent was by no means unique in having many assisted emigrants but it did have more than many counties, in particular many left the Wealden area of the county. The motives of the emigrants were a mixture of fleeing from a distressing situation and hope of advancement in their new country.

Emigrants from the county who were given financial assistance were only a small proportion of a far larger number of Kentish people who emigrated in search of a better life without the need of any financial assistance. Those people set off having made all arrangements themselves; their story is not told in this book. Nor is the story told of those who had to leave the country because they were transported, condemned by the courts to transportation to Australia. Rather this is the story of people such as John Stroud.

John Stroud was born in the village of Egerton in 1814, the son of a carrier. Egerton lies close to Pluckley in the heart of the county. As a boy John was employed as a farm labourer, suffering the great hardships of all agricultural labourers in Kent at that time. He later said of that time that he *'fain would have filled his belly with the husks that the swine did eat'*.[2] He was bitter about the way that the landed gentry treated their workers and longed for a country with more freedom and equality. John, a tall strong man, became a brick maker employed on Lord Stanhope's estate at Chevening where bricks were made for the estate properties.

He married Ellen Blundell daughter of the estate steward and they were housed in an estate cottage. After much heart-searching they decided to emigrate to Australia with their little daughter Amy in order to make a better life for themselves. It was a great wrench to leave behind the beautiful countryside they knew so well, but above all it was painful to leave their relatives and friends.

In 1853 they embarked for Australia, their passage paid for by the parish. They took with them John's father's Bible, a most treasured possession. The voyage took six months during which Ellen was constantly sick; keeping

---

[2] East, Sir Ronald A family who's who, (1976)

alive on hard ship's biscuits soaked in brandy. Eventually they arrived in Hobart, Tasmania, and on their first Sunday there, attended the Melville Street Methodist church and were invited home for dinner. Ellen never forgot this hospitality. It was the first real meal she had been able to eat since leaving England.

From Hobart their ship took a week to reach Sydney where they boarded a paddle steamer bound for Melbourne, taking another week. Here they settled at Fitzroy where there was plenty of work to be had for a young brick maker. They were devout Methodists and attended the Rose Street Methodist church. John was for many years Sunday school superintendent and would walk miles delivering religious tracts.

It was the time of the gold rush and John could not resist going off to try his luck. He was lucky and came back with enough money to buy a small quarry and start his own brick making business in Albert Street, Brunswick. The business did well for that part of Victoria was expanding rapidly due to the gold mining and there was a large demand for housing.

Although several of their twelve children had died in infancy, there was no doubt in Ellen and John's minds that they had made the right decision in leaving England.

The way in which John and Ellen Stroud seized the opportunities before them in their new homeland epitomises the stories of many of the emigrants in the pages that follow.

In Kent they had no standing, few opportunities and less money, but they had the courage and enterprise to leave and make a new life for themselves and their children.

John and Ellen Stroud in old age
(Courtesy of Andy Straw)

The situation in Kent 1815 - 1835

The population of Kent shot up by 56% between 1801 and 1831, infant mortality was going down and people were marrying younger, as a result there was no longer enough work to go round. When the Napoleonic Wars ended, and English agriculture fell into deep depression, the farm labourers were the worst sufferers. All over Kent able-bodied men were no longer able to support their families on the wages they received, and many also suffered periods of unemployment. Farmers were paying 12 shillings a week which was not a living wage. Rented cottages cost two or three pounds a year. A large loaf could cost eight pence and meat the same or more a pound.

William Cobbett rode through Kent in 1821 when writing his 'Rural Rides.' He observed that the county was 'in an extremely unsatisfactory state and has certainly a greater mass of suffering to endure than any other part of the kingdom.'[3]

It had become the norm for farm workers to be employed by the week or day as required and this could mean near starvation in the winter when the farmers had no work to offer. During the war the practice of unmarried farm workers living in the farm house and having their meals with the family had virtually died out. Cobbett thought this was because it was cheaper to pay low wages than provide meals.

---

[3] Cobbett W, *Rural Rides*, 1912 edition, vol 1 p 46

In addition there was a growing use of threshing machines, which were hated by the workers, since they had relied upon hand threshing to provide them with winter work. In 1829 Kent magistrates sent a letter to the Duke of Wellington, then the Prime Minister, to let him know the plight of the poor in the county. The letter was published in the Maidstone Journal in December. It tells of:

'the deep and unprecedented distress, which from our personal and local knowledge we are enabled to state, prevails among all classes throughout the county, to a degree that must not only be ruinous to the interests of individuals but must also at no distant period, be attended with serious consequences to the national prosperity.'[4]

Farm labourers who were in work were given money and bread to supplement their low wages so that they could support their families. 'This system of relief', wrote an anonymous freeholder to Sir Edward Knatchbull, M.P, J.P. and chairman of the magistrates at the East Kent Sessions, 'breaks the spirit of the Poor ... and is one of the crying evils of the day.'[5]

There had been unrest in the county from 1827, made worse by bad harvests in 1828 and 1829, and this led up to the Swing Riots of 1830-1, which began in Kent and spread to the southern and southwestern counties of England. They were known as the Swing Riots because farmers received threatening letters signed 'Captain Swing,' although no leader claiming the name was ever

---

[4] Maidstone Journal, Dec 22 1829
[5] CKS U95 / C14 / 2

discovered. There was no organised plot, the cause of these spontaneous outbreaks of lawlessness lay in specific grievances related to the worsening lifestyle of the farm labourers who were already at subsistence level. The riots consisted of machine breaking, rioting and arson. In August 1830 there were a number of cases of machine breaking in East Kent and more in September and October across the county.

The Justices of the Peace of East Kent met with other gentlemen in Canterbury to 'take into consideration the disturbed state of this County and to adopt such measures as may be deemed necessary to preserve the public peace.'[6] They decided to offer a reward for the discovery of the identity of the machine breakers and they agreed to the swearing in of special constables. Some of those in authority within the county such as Sir Edward Knatchbull of Brabourne were not without sympathy for the labourers. On the whole though, the large farmers, who were most threatened by the riots were the least sympathetic. At the Quarter Sessions in Canterbury the rioters pleaded guilty and instead of the possible seven years transportation received four days in prison and some paternalistic advice from Sir Edward. The Home Secretary disapproved of the light sentences and at later trials they were far harsher. Over Kent as a whole, 100 men were tried, four were executed for arson, 48 imprisoned, 52 transported and 25 acquitted.

---

[6] NA HO 52 / 8 XC / A 16847

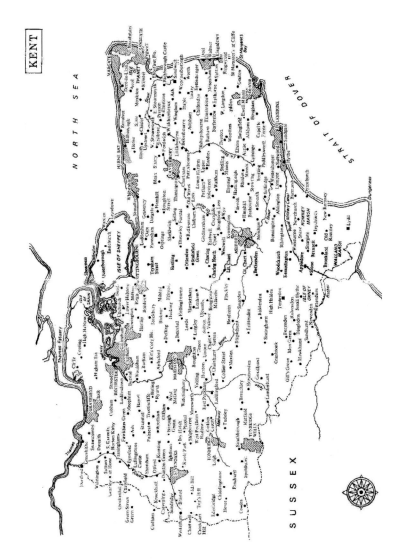

Matters were bad across the county; in the Sittingbourne area, after the firing of a farmhouse in the parish of Borden, affairs rapidly worsened to the extent that the justices found it necessary to call in a troop of the 7th Dragoons from Canterbury. A farm at neighbouring

Stockbury was burned down and large groups of workers assembled at Wormshill and Newington demanding increased pay. The Stockbury rioters numbered about 200 and cheered as the farmhouse burnt to the ground. The Rev. Poore, rector of Murston, and Justice of the Peace reported to the Home Secretary that a large body of men had assembled at Stockbury, *'with two flags one Black and the other tricolour,'* and were approaching Sittingbourne after pausing for refreshment at the Squirrels Inn when the troops were called upon to disperse them.

'The result was the Rioters dispersed as they heard of our Advance and they have directed their revolutionary proceedings in the opposite direction.'[7] The leader was unknown in the neighbourhood. On October 26th incendiaries had burnt two barns near Faversham, that day the Maidstone Journal reported:

'Between eight and nine o'clock on Tuesday morning about 300 labourers, armed with sticks appeared in the village of Lenham..they were preceded by a flag or banner. This riotous band after terrifying the inhabitants of Lenham for three or four hours, proceeded towards Hollingbourne. On their way thither they met the Earl of Winchelsea, who was on the road to his seat. The noble earl alighted from his carriage and addressed the insurgents, cautioning them to desist from illegal proceedings, and to disperse peaceably. He seconded his admonition by giving the men three guineas. They did not however, obey the noble earl's salutary advice, as they proceeded on their march towards Hollingbourne, and, on their

---

[7] ibid.

arriving there, some assistance was rendered to them by the inhabitants.

You may be struck by the lack of violence against the earl, but the men were not out to inflict harm on others but to gain a living wage for themselves.

In the same week at Ospringe, a gang of machine breakers forced other labourers to stop work and accompany them. On the 28th about 100 labourers marched round Hollingbourne demanding 2s 6d a day for married men and two shillings for every single man. One of the Hollingbourne farmers, told them they could not agree to these demands.

On October 30th the Rev John Poore, was writing to Sir Edward Knatchbull M.P. with information not only about his own area around Sittingbourne but also around Maidstone. Speaking of the previous day he wrote : *'The aspect of affairs in the Neighbourhood of Maidstone is most gloomy...a large body rose begging contributions at Langly Heath and its vicinity. Some say the number 500 others 700. Another body at Lenham of 300 and similar number on Tunbridge side...the magistrates had been employed in swearing in special constables and had resolved on marching with Sir J. Brown and the military to Langly for the purpose of dispersing the Rioters and if possible seize the ringleaders.'*[8] That same day the magistrates rode out from Maidstone with soldiers and the mayor to meet the rioters. When they refused to go home the Riot Act was read, then the ringleaders were arrested, placed in a carriage and escorted to Maidstone goal by the cavalry. The labourers

[8] CKS U951/C14

17

then dispersed. At no time during the disturbances in Kent did the troops fire on rioters.

At the end of October 1830 the Kentish magistrates established a patrol of special constables on foot and horse in every parish. They were to report any person out at an unreasonable hour or arrest them there and then. In November West Kent was affected by rioting and machine breaking and by the 17th George Douglas, a Maidstone gentleman was writing to the Home Secretary in great agitation: *'I beg leave to remind you that we are in this most Disturbed part of the county of Kent without any military protection. The 7th Dragoons left Lenham upon the disturbances in London of the 5th…we want a few soldiers to keep down the dissatisfied and daring spirit of the country people. Their wages have been raised here to 2/3d which they appeared to be satisfied with for a short time but they now want 2/6d. It appears nothing will content them…we might well be murdered here before assistance could be had.'*[9]

March 1831 brought further arson and machine breaking in East Kent and Romney Marsh. In June landowners and tenant farmers from ten neighbouring villages, and Sittingbourne, met and resolved unanimously to form an association for the protection of property, to keep the peace, and pay rewards for the arrest of incendiaries.[10] Regular patrols were taking place at Ashford and Faversham.

However in 1831, after the savage sentences passed in all affected counties, the revolt died away leaving the

[9] NA HO 52 / 8
[10] CKS U840 / 0236 / 9

condition of the labourers largely unchanged, yet the problems of unemployment and poverty had not gone away. Some farmers raised the wages of their labourers to two shillings and six pence a day; and, certainly, threshing machines generally went out of use for some years in the county.[11]

In the aftermath of Swing, Kent parishes devised ways of creating jobs for their labourers to keep them occupied and paid. In the parish of Stockbury where there had been a good deal of unrest, a vestry meeting was held in 1832 at which it was agreed that all occupiers of land would *'constantly employ one labourer of 21 or over for every £35 for which they were assessed'*.[12] All the parish labourers not employed in this way were known as 'supernumery' and the rate for their relief was to be one shilling and three pence a day for those aged over 21 with less for those who were younger.

In truth the situation in the parish was desperate, for there were so many families without work or means of support and the rates were insufficient to meet their needs. This 'roundsman' system of dealing with unemployment was widely used in the county. Labourers were sent to work on the farms in a parish and their wages subsidised by the rates. In some parishes labourers were directly employed by the parish on road repairs or in a workshop run by the parish. Staplehurst was one of those where a workshop was set up for men to produce sacks, bags and leather goods and Cranbrook had a parish farm. In some Kent parishes it was alleged

[11] Cresswell A., The Swing riots in Kent, (2003)
[12] CKS P348 /8/ 1

that farmers no longer had regular workers, because they could get men when they needed them from the parish overseers at a shilling a day.[13]

In Stockbury there were 23 heads of household who were in such need that they could not feed themselves unless the parish paid all or part of their rent. James Burr's rent was £5 and he was allowed £2 towards it, William Beaumont's rent was £5 of which £4 was allowed, Richard Whitehead's was £4, of which £2 was allowed. The poor also came to the vestry asking for clothing and coal. In May 1833 James Kitney applied for a pair of trousers, a pair of shoes, a round frock, (that is a stout smock to wear for work), and two shirts for his boy. He was given assistance for half of his needs. Such scenarios were being repeated all over Kent.

During September 1833 nine of the Stockbury poor applied for their rent to be paid. None were granted all of it, most were given part and all were told that no rents could be paid in future. In the past the parish had paid part of William Whitehead senior's rent. He had four children the youngest eleven years old. This time he was refused and told he would be refused again in the future. James Syflet however was disabled and had four children so his whole rent was paid.

Inevitably tempers ran high and that month 'The overseer Mr Brittenden having been greatly insulted by two of the paupers William Beaumont and James Rayfield, it was agreed

---

[13] Lansberry, F, Government & politics in Kent 1640-1914, (2001)

he should represent the case to the magistrates without delay with a view to their being punished.'

December 1833 brought many applications for clothing from the villagers as the weather grew colder. It was agreed that coal should be bought by the farmers, to be sold to the poor who applied for firing at a reduced price. Nearly a year later in October 1834 the situation was still as desperate with 18 applications for rent and clothes, many of which were refused.

Large numbers of agricultural workers in the southeast were pauperised and reliant on relief. The able bodied unemployed poor had become the largest group of those needing relief. Kent was spending high sums on poor relief in proportion to its population.[14] This was partly due to the large population in the metropolitan north west of the county but there were also agricultural areas of great poverty in the south west of the county and the Weald. There were wide variations within the county in the amount spent by parishes on the poor.

The Poor Law Amendment Act was passed in 1834 requiring parishes to group together in unions to build joint workhouses for their destitute. Thus substantial workhouse buildings began to go up all over the country. The idea of workhouses was not a new one. Each parish had long been responsible for its own poor and some were housed in small workhouses established in the 18th century, whilst most were given out-relief as we have seen in Stockbury. Before the 1834 Act, the

---

14 Melling E, The poor- Kentish sources IV, (1964)

churchwardens and overseers of every parish levied their own rates to relieve the poor and organised their relief within the parish.

The 1834 Act aimed to stop all out-relief to the able-bodied on the principle that if they were fit they should be able to maintain themselves and if they could not then they must enter the workhouse. Upon arrival they would be separated from their families and given backbreaking work to do. The new workhouses were to act as a deterrent; a warning to those whom the gentry and farmers saw as the undeserving poor. The act also had the opposing aim of providing a place of refuge for the sick and the disabled. The two aims were to prove difficult to achieve together.

So now the poor of Kent had a new fear, that they would be sent to the workhouse and separated from their families. Small wonder then that for some of the more enterprising, emigration offered a solution and a way to keep their self-respect.

In fact a number of Kentish parishes had already begun to help their poorest inhabitants to emigrate as early as the 1820s using money from the poor rate.

Assisted emigration in Kent before the Poor Law Act

Assisted emigration on a small scale had begun in Kent a few years before the Swing Riots. Headcorn was the first parish to assist labourers to emigrate, in 1824. They sent about 20 emigrants a year to America from 1824 at a cost of £8 a head.[15] The poor rate steadily declined as a result and by 1827 they estimated that if another ten families left, the parish could find work for all the rest.

Thomas Law Hodges, MP for West Kent and chairman of the West Kent Quarter Sessions, was enthusiastic about emigration. He told the select Committee on Emigration in 1826 that his own parish of Benenden had financed the passage of 27 villagers to New York at a cost of £13-10 per adult. This sum was made up of ten guineas for passage and provisions, and a few shillings for landing fees. A few more shillings were needed for carriage from Benenden to the London docks and two sovereigns to be given on arrival in New York. He personally lent over £1000 to the parish to send another 145 emigrants to America in 1827 and 1828.[16]

Hodges described to the Lords Committee of 1831 how emigration had affected the parish:

---

[15] Yates, Hume & Hastings, Religion & society in Kent 1640-1914, (1994)
[16] Johnston H, British emigration policy 1815-30, (1972)

23

'I found the parish burdened with a number of persons who couldn't get employment at any part of the year; and when the autumn came and throughout the winter, there were from 30 to 80 persons out of work in the parish. In the course of two years 149 persons emigrated to America, men, women and children; and in consequence of that we now have comparatively but few persons out of work, and our poor-rates have materially decreased. During a great part of the years 1825-26 there were from 70 to 80 able-bodied men on the parish books for want of employ. Since 56 of them have emigrated it is a rare circumstance to have any out of work except in severe weather.'

In Hodges' evidence to the select committee in 1826 he had also spoken of neighbouring Cranbrook where of the 290 agricultural labourers there was *'an excess nearly all the year round unemployed or at least for whom no regular farming work can be obtained; for 50 of the 290.'* Hodges told the committee that eleven single men and one married couple had emigrated to America in the previous week from Cranbrook.

Nearby, in the parish of Woodchurch he said there were 64 men out of work. He reported that Smarden had tried emigration already, for there the population had soared from 600 to over 1000 in the previous forty years. In 1824 27 people had been assisted to New York and a similar number had paid their own way. Others in the parish were planning to go because *'reports constantly arriving from them contain the most favourable accounts of their welfare so much so that almost all the labourers of that parish are desirous of going to America.'*[17]

---

[17] Weller M, Bygone Kent vol 14, Emigration from Kent, part one

Other Kentish parishes followed; including Marden, Tenterden, Headcorn, Westerham, Deal, Holden, Northbourne, Mongeham, Sevenoaks, Thanet and Chatham. [18]

Sometimes a man managed to get himself to America leaving his family behind, dependent on the parish, in the hope that they would be helped to emigrate to join him. This happened to Benjamin Cotton's family. He got to America and his wife and seven children were admitted to Cranbrook parish workhouse costing the parish twelve shillings a week. When Mrs Cotton received a letter from her husband in America asking them all to come, she appealed to the parish for the fare.[19] It made economic sense to agree to spend the £50 to send the family rather than support them for what could have been many years.

At Sandhurst, a parish with a population of 850, there had been an enormous increase upon the few hundred pounds a year paid in poor relief a generation earlier. During the early 1820s something like £2000 a year was paid.[20] In March 1826 at a public vestry meeting at the Swan Inn, it was agreed to raise money to *'enable persons who are chargeable to the parish and desirous to Emigrate to America'* to go. £150 was to be raised by a loan at 5%

---

[18] Johnston H, British emigration policy 1815-30, (1972)
[19] CKS P100 / 8 / 2
[20] Holmes N, Emigration to the United States of America from Sandhurst, Arch Cant vol 73

interest paid from the poor rate.[21] Two local men loaned the money to the parish.

The records of Sandhurst are unusual in that so much has survived to inform us of their emigrants' preparations for the journey. The first requests to emigrate were recorded in the vestry book in 1822 when three men asked to go with their families to America. However no action was taken until four years later. In 1826 the men of the vestry heard that Benenden, the adjoining parish, had sent some poor villagers to America and this encouraged them to do the same. Three families and three single men wanted to leave in 1826 and in the event twelve adults, five children and two babies went.

The churchwardens and overseers made the arrangements; they consulted with Benenden parish officers and wrote letters to London shipping agents. [22] Several letters passed between the Sandhurst churchwarden John Hilder and the London agent.

This is one of the agent James Chapman's letters to John Hilder:

'Sir

I have to acknowledge the receipt of your favor of the 27th inst. And according to your instructions have engaged passage for seven men, three women and seven children including two at the breast, which go free. Observe what you state respecting my adding some Butter and Cheese for the children and

---

[21] CKS P321 / 8 / 1
[22] CKS P321 / 28 / F / 2

Women; this I shall not object to. In answer to what other stores it will be necessary for the Voyage, they will require Bedding which if they have not got you will have to purchase for them, as well as plates and dishes, knives and forks a few saucepans & yes some of the parishes allow them Tea and Sugar & other small stores. Should you feel disposed to allow them the above stores with the Bedding, probably you would wish to know the whole expense which would then amount to Four pounds five shillings each person. The ship Virginia by which the passengers are to sail will leave London on the 15th May they ought therefore to be in Town on the 13th. I shall be glad to hear from you stating which day you mean the passengers to be in London also if I am to procure the Bedding and the extra provisions. I remain sir

Your faithfully James Chapman'[23]

Arrangements were made rapidly, for in each of three years the emigrants were on board ship within two months of the decision being made to send them.

The Sandhurst parish records tell us something about the individuals who so bravely set off to the other side of the world; Charles Wenban was 29 in 1826 when he and his young wife decided to join the group of emigrants. Charles was the eldest of a family of ten and three of his brothers followed him to America in the 1827 group. Charles was a close friend of James and Mary Harris, two of the other 1826 emigrants for he had been one of the witnesses at their wedding a few years previously, the Harris's were accompanied by their two young children.

---

[23] CKS P321 / 16 / 9

George Fuller and his wife Jemima were to go with their four children and baby. George had applied to go to America twice before. To prepare for their new life the Fuller family children were vaccinated against smallpox as were other families the following year.[24]

George Wybourn was only 15 when he joined the 1826 emigrants; the eldest of a family of ten children. His family had been constantly requesting help from the parish for clothes and food and fuel. The rest of the family followed George to America in 1828. Five more single young men made up the 1826 group - Samuel Simmonds, David Smith, George Smith, William Harris and John Mainard.

These emigrants sailed in the *Virginia* from London. The cost was £7 for adults and half for children under 14.[25] The fare was somewhat less for the two later groups. Provisions for those sailing on the *Virginia* were ordered from the London agent with the parish providing dishes and saucepans. The provisions ordered consisted of 224lbs of salt beef which was a barrel full, 200lbs of salt pork, 85lbs of bacon, 896lbs of best brown bread, baked as hard as biscuit, 784 lbs of potatoes, 56 lbs of flour, 14lbs of rice and split peas. John Hilder the Sandhurst churchwarden, insisted on adding 26lbs of butter and 36lbs of cheese. A receipt shows he also bought tea, coffee, sugar and soap in London to add to the goods already sent on board.[26] Added to this a little receipt shows that six knives forks and spoons were bought,

---

[24] CKS P321 / 12 / B / 3
[25] ibid
[26] ibid

together with vinegar salt and pepper. All of this amounted to over £45. The emigrants from Sandhurst were most generously provided for by their thoughtful neighbours and their health during the voyage and upon arrival would have been all the better for it. It is clear that in Sandhurst the motive of the ratepayers was not only to save money on the rates in the future but to give the emigrants a good start in their new lives.

As soon as they reached the London docks the group boarded ship. Meanwhile John Hilder collected the cash, changing around £23 into dollars in order to give each family a little cash for their arrival. The single men got the equivalent of about thirty shillings each, and the families more according to the number of children so that the Fuller family were given £7. Mr Hilder paid the captain the passage money-£101; his signed receipt survives. After farewells were said he could go home reflecting that he had done all a man could to ensure that the Sandhurst group's new start in life went as well as possible. Without John Hilder the villagers could have fallen prey to dishonest people, for there were always some waiting around the docks offering to change money or put emigrants up until they could board ship.

In 1826 the average sailing time from London to New York was between 30 and 40 days but without favourable winds it could take far longer.

A larger group left Sandhurst for America in 1827; three married couples with large families and five single men. To equip them for their new life the parish gave all the emigrants in this group between £1 and 30 shillings a head. The whole bundle of receipts for their goods survives.[27] The Wenban brothers were all literate and able to write their own requests for clothes. Charles Wenban asked for a pair of blankets, two men's stockings, two women's stockings, three yards of flannel, two yards of another colour of flannel, trousers and some print fabric. Each family ordered fabric by the yard, which the women would have made up during the voyage into the required garments. Everyone ordered boots. John Lavender requested sheets and blankets, a pair of shoes, a pair of stockings and two changes of clothes for every member of the family. He could write but his spelling was poor as was Henry Sivyer's. Henry wanted a round frock, which was a working smock. James Harris requested a waistcoat and stockings.

Good reports of their new lives in America must have come back to Sandhurst for in 1828, £250 was raised for a third and even larger group to leave. The emigrants consisted of two families; John Wybourn his wife and seven children and Stephen Swatland his wife and five children. Stephen Swatland was one of those parishioners who were then having their rent paid by the parish. Again all of the receipts and bills survive, giving a vivid picture of the preparations for their emigration. The Swatland family chose to equip themselves with materials to make up shoes, a counterpane and yards of bed ticking as well as a Guernsey (a thick jumper).[28] The receipt for the Wybourns shows that they decided on plenty of calico, worsted and print fabric, buttons, thread and twist as well as yards of flannel all in all a total of £4.

---

[27] CKS P321 / 12 / B/ 24
[28] ibid

The bill for the supplies for the Wybourn and Swatland families.

[With kind permission of the Centre for Kentish Studies]

The Wybourn family had been a constant drain on the parish resources. Two of their children had died in the 1820s and their second son John was mentally unstable. He had been in a home at Ticehurst at the expense of the parish for months at a time in 1825 and 1827. By May 1827 he was 'improved in his state of mind' and returned to Sandhurst in August.

In each of the three years the parish hired a waggoner and his waggon pulled by four horses, to take the emigrants and their luggage to London. In 1826 bills show the young single men were given five shillings each to get to London, although in the following years all members of the party travelled together. Each family sailing from London was allowed two trunks or chests but those who left from Liverpool were only allowed 28lbs per person free on the passage from London to Liverpool. The parish paid for over 1232 lbs extra for the 1827 group.

The second and third groups sailed from Liverpool in the *Hercules*; and the *London* respectively.

John Hilder travelled separately by coach to London, to see that arrangements went smoothly in both 1826 and 1827 and another churchwarden Mr Humphry went in 1828. The 1827 and 1828 groups who departed from Liverpool were left in London at Pickford's wharf. It was here, at the Basin, City Road, London, where the emigrants of Sandhurst and Benenden met up to travel to Liverpool together by barge on the canal. A letter between the overseers of Sandhurst and Benenden shows anxiety about meeting up in good time:

'I have received a letter from Pickford this morning in which he strongly recommends the parties to be at his wharf (City Road) on Saturday instead of Monday and we have arranged for our team to be there precisely at 11 o'clock Saturday and I hope you will take care to get your team off so that they may reach the wharf punctually at the above hour.

William Lansdell (To Mr Humphrey)'[29]

The emigrants were provided with an allowance of a shilling per day per adult and six pence per child for the six-day journey to Liverpool. The fares were 16 shillings each for the adults by canal.[30] This was how Pickford's, the modern removal firm started.

On arrival in Liverpool they were met by an agent who took charge of them until it was time to go on board which was not for several days.

A problem arose in 1828. The Liverpool agent gave the emigrants their landing money in sterling rather than dollars and this proved too great a temptation for John Wibourn. The Benenden overseer wrote to Mr Humphrey:

'I received advice from Liverpool this morning and am sorry to say that Wibourn after the muster and payment of premiums and passage on deck on the 20th left with William Wenman, (a Benenden man), and went on shore saying that they would

[29] CKS P321 / 16 / 9
[30] CKS P321 / 12 / B 24

return again after a pint or two of porter in time before the vessel sailed. However they did not return before the morning of the next day, such unwarrantable conduct is unpardonable. Mrs Wibourn has the premium with the exception of a few shillings with which it appears he got intoxicated, under all the circumstances our agent thought it advisable to secure a passage in the 'Peru' which will sail about the 25th but they will be attended with an extra expense-but as the men appear very desirous to go I think it is the best course he could take particularly in the case of Wibourn. The other is a single man and it is very unfortunate circumstance that two drunken fellows should have taken their passage on the same vessel.'[31]

Mrs Wybourn must have been beside herself because her husband missed the sailing, unless she felt she was well rid of him. In fact Wybourn did sail in the *Peru* though whether he ever rejoined his family in New York is unknown.

Shipping companies had seen by 1829, that it was worth their while to send advertisements to parishes offering contracts to take the poor as passengers.[32] An example survives amongst the parish records of Preston-next-Wingham, it is a printed letter from Parkin Browne and Co. of Threadneedle Street. 'We are ready to contract for the conveyance of paupers to North America. If London is too distant a ship can call at the nearest safe port if there are a sufficient number.' Another example is a hand

---

[31] ibid
[32] CCA U3 / 245 / 16 / 70

written letter to the parish officers of Headcorn from a Captain Reynolds at Dover:[33]

Rough seas caused chaos at meal times. [Illustrated London News 12 Feb 1887]

'Gentlemen,

Having a brig about 182 tons that will be ready to sail for Quebec at the middle of next month, I shall be obliged by the favour of an early answer informing me if you have any poor persons you would wish to send out from your parish as possible settlers. Adult's passage £4-10s, children under 12, £2-5s.'

---

[33] CKS P181 / 18 / 27

Biddenden parish began, in a small way, to help their poor to emigrate in 1826 when they gave one George Relf £5 towards emigrating to America. In 1827 a further six people were supported to America their fares paid and their provisions bought. Their carriage to London from Kent and passage to Liverpool were paid and on landing they were given £10 between them. In all it cost the parish over £50.[34] Another eleven were sent to America that year. In 1828 they decided that seven people would be selected from the list of those waiting to go to America and the money found for them to go.[35] In 1830 the overseers were authorised by the parish to send people from time to time as they applied, provided the committee approved of them, and their passage was to be paid for from the poor rate. In March 1831 agreement was reached to send *'certain persons maintained in the parish distress book'*. Samuel Paine, his wife and two children were allowed to go in March 1833 along with others whose names are not mentioned in the parish records. Biddenden continued in this way after the Poor Law Act was passed.

A special vestry meeting was held at Egerton in 1827 to discuss sending several families to America. It was agreed to raise £130 for the purpose.[36] They thought it would be encouraging to know how much money they were saving by sending the families so: *'We also order that the names of each family so emigrated be regularly entered into the weekly relief book of the parish at the rate of 6/- for each week for each family that sum being considered by the vestry to*

[34] CKS P26/12/6
[35] CKS P26 / 8 / 1
[36] CKS P78B / 8 / 3

equal the amount of what each family would cost provided they was at home.'

Assisted emigration from Westerham began in 1831 when a public vestry meeting was held and it was agreed *'it will be advisable and beneficial to the parish to defray the expense of the passage of William Burnett his wife and seven of their children to America out of the poor rates.'*[37] The churchwardens were to act with 'as little expense as possible'. So no doubt they would have enquired for the cheapest passage. There is nothing to show that they gave money on landing, unlike Sandhurst. On the other hand the Westerham parish workhouse did serve a hot dinner every day and had spent over £600 in 1831/2 on the poor in the parish.[38] The vestry carefully calculated the long-term benefit to the village ratepayers when they decided to help Robert Smith, his wife and seven children to go to Canada in 1832. Over the previous four years the family had cost the parish around £133 inside the workhouse and in poor relief in their home, and in view of this, £48 in fares and £19 for the onward journey to Upper Canada from Quebec was a bargain. Three years later young John Smith, another of Robert's sons was assisted to join the family in Canada since he was also finding it difficult to get work.

In the wake of the Swing Riots parish vestries continued to encourage emigration which they saw as a cheaper option in the long-term than supporting poor families on the rates. In 1832 paupers were assisted to America from Bredgar, Rochester, Wateringbury, East Malling and

---

[37] CKS P389 / 8/ 1
[38] ibid

Chart Sutton. Chart Sutton parish had borrowed £100 to *'emigrate the surplus poor to America'* whilst East Malling that year raised double the amount. [39]

That same year the Faversham vestry decided it was *'advisable to encourage the emigration of such Paupers as may be willing to go to the British Settlements in North America.'*[40] However as reported in the Maidstone Journal of April:

'The encouragement held out to emigrants to induce them to leave this town for Upper Canada has entirely failed, for although about 20 of the labouring class had expressed a desire to depart from their native country, as soon as means were ascertained to be forth coming, their hearts sickened at the thought of leaving their country and connexions, and they determined to remain in Old England, notwithstanding the inducements which have been held out to them.''[41]

This must have happened to many people; they realised they could well be better off abroad but could not bear the thought of leaving England, home and loved ones, or taking the risks involved in such a long journey.

1833 found a small group of the poor of neighbouring Ospringe setting off to embark for North America at Gravesend.[42]

---

[39] CKS P83 / 12 / 5
[40] CCA / U3 / 146 / 8 / 4
[41] Maidstone Journal, Apr 10th 1832
[42] CCA U3 / 123 / 12 / 36

The journey to the port [Illustrated London News 21 December 1844]

Such emigration schemes were not without their critics; William Cobbett was one, he felt that if English agriculture was properly organised there would be no need for farm workers to emigrate. His criticism was justified in that many people were encouraged to emigrate for no better reason than to reduce the rates. Cobbett argued in 1830 that the poor had a right to live in England and a right to relief.[43] It should be remembered that the very people who benefited from encouraging the poor to emigrate were those on the parish vestries.

---

[43] Cobbett W, William Cobbett's Weekly Political Register, 13 Mar 1830

A small receipt survives amongst the Headcorn parish records, just a scrap of paper:

'Receive of the parish of Headcorn the sum of £3-10s for the purpose of clearing myself and family from the parish, and to emigrate to New South Whales (sic), and I do hereby agree not to be chargeable any more from this time to the parish of Headcorn as witness my hand

Jesse Stephens X'[44]

How harsh the overseer's phrase *'clearing myself and my family from the parish'* is, as if the Stephens were so much rubbish to be got rid of. Indeed this was the attitude of some of the landowners. Occasionally another view is heard. The view that the country might actually need these poor people:

St John's vestry Margate, concluded in 1836 *'the encouragement of Emigration is in principle erroneous and in effect is opposed to the best interests and safety of the Nation-in as much as thereby the Country is drained of the only legitimate source of strength and importance namely its industrious population and that therefore this vestry will not sanction it.'*[45]

As we have seen this was not the general view of vestries in Kent.

---

[44] CKS P181 / 18 / 27
[45] CCA U3 / 140 / 8 / 2

It is estimated that Kent lost 15,000 people by emigration during 1830-1 and yet its population continued to climb.[46]

We have seen that there were wide differences in the way that parishes had proceeded and the amount of money they had spent on their emigrants. All this was to be standardised by the Poor Law Commissioners after the Poor Law Act of 1834.

---

[46] Yates, Hume & Hastings, Religion & society in Kent, (1994)

The Poor Law Commissioners & emigration 1835 - 1855

The Poor Law Amendment Act of 1834 brought about the setting up of the Poor Law Commission and the union workhouses. In parts of Kent there were riots in protest at the change in the system; particularly the curtailing of out-relief.

The act included a clause enabling parishes to raise money for emigration. Straight away the commissioners interested themselves in promoting emigration. A complete system was put in place to make it as straight forward as possible for poor people to emigrate and to iron out the variations in the arrangements that parishes had been making for themselves.

Parish funds were now to be raised with the sanction of the Commissioners to clothe and equip poor families and to take them to the ports and provide them with a little money to keep them going until they got work.

The Commissioners first annual report, published in 1835, recorded that although all the new poor law unions had been supplied with instructions as to how to 'rid themselves of surplus pauper labourers,' by enabling them to emigrate, scant use had been made of the system in the first year. Only 320 people from the whole of England had been assisted to emigrate in this way and had embarked for Canada or the United States.

From Kent just nine had gone, all from the parish of Aldington to Canada. This great drop in numbers leaving can be explained by the fact that the officials at parish level had to familiarise themselves with the new legislation and see what it would mean in practical terms as far as emigration went. Matters had now to be carried forward through the auspices of the new poor law unions.

The Commissioner's instructions were laid out in a circular sent to the union workhouses in May of that year. They allowed the ratepayers of a parish to raise or borrow funds not exceeding half the yearly rate for the preceding three years. The permission of the Commissioners was required before any particular scheme went ahead and the money had to be repaid by the ratepayers within five years. If the money was borrowed it could either be from individuals or from the Exchequer Bill Loan Commissioners.

Should any of the poor who had agreed to emigrate change their minds, after expenses had been incurred, then the money was to be somehow recouped from them. A big change was that their destination had to be a British colony and as we have seen, before the act, America was the favoured destination of assisted emigrants. The Poor Law Commissioners did not sanction emigration to America. In their 8th report they noted that in some instances men had made their own way there and then their families had applied to the parish for help to join them. However since America was no longer a colony they expressed their 'strong opinion of the great inexpediency of rendering assistance to the families of persons so circumstanced.'

Contracts now had to be made to convey emigrants to a port as directed by the Agent General for Emigration.

The contract included the maintenance and medical attendance of the emigrants during migration and also a provision that upon arrival at least £2 would be paid to the head of each family and £1 to single people.

It was soon found necessary to tighten regulations, as in some cases, costs incurred were considered excessive. The amended regulations meant that the emigration money was paid to the union treasurer, then half of it to the shipping contractor ten days after the ship had sailed and the rest after the voyage was over. Churchwardens and overseers were not to spend more than three pence a mile per person in taking emigrants to the port. Clothing worth £1 per adult could be given by parish vestries to the emigrants, and £2 worth if they were going east of the Cape of Good Hope.

In the early days some emigrants had been defrauded of their supplies for the voyage, but now exactly what each person on the ship must be supplied with was laid down. The Commissioners had been asked to allow the emigrants to take their own provisions on board but had refused because in their opinion:

'Individuals who avail themselves of parish assistance to emigrate are seldom of prudent and economical habits; and being inexperienced in everything related to shipping, they are not persons who can safely be entrusted with the custody of provisions and stores for the voyage. Having been unaccustomed to relying on their own resources they are careless of their stores, and frequently waste in a few days the stock put on board for as many weeks... In other instances where emigrants have had money given them to provide stores it has been thoughtlessly squandered in spirits...'

Shockingly, eleven emigrants actually starved to death on the voyage to America from Liverpool in 1837 on board the *Diamond*. Evidence given by surviving passengers and by crew showed they had hardly any provisions at all and one had none. Under the new contract it was in the interests of the contractor to perform the voyage as rapidly as possible although inevitably the weather could cause considerable delays.

Edward Tufnell the Assistant Poor Law Commissioner for Kent and East Sussex wrote in his report on the year 1837-38, that the year

'has been for the most part one of peculiar hardship as respects the labouring classes during the past year, arising from causes which can have but slight effect in other parts of England.'[47]

The reason was that hop prices had crashed putting some growers out of business whilst corn prices were high. The employers did not have the usual amount of work. Tufnell knew that many felt out-relief was the obvious solution but he was strongly opposed to going back to this. He felt the destitution of those who had been involved in hop growing was likely to be permanent and that the way forward was to decrease the population. The Weald was a hop growing area and so provided many of the emigrants.

Luckily a new way of assisting emigration to Australia by means of the sale of 'waste colonial lands' was formed. The money from the land sales paid the passage

[47] 4th annual report of the Poor Law Commissioners

leaving the parishes to provide only the transport to the port, clothing, and a small sum on landing.

'The agents for the new colony at Spencer's Gulf have been collecting emigrants and about 9 or 10 ships have sailed from Kent and East Sussex for Australia in 1837-8, taking labourers to a place where wages are nearly double.'

Tufnell had heard of labourers who had gone out in 1837 and found excellent prospects.

The winter of 1837-8 was unusually severe in Kent bringing heavy snow and overwhelming the new system of no out-relief. At the Faversham Union in January 1838 the building was full and out-relief was given to 257 heads of families, of which 139 were in the parish of Faversham alone, who with their families amounted to 549 individuals. The majority were engaged in the oyster fishery, which the frost had brought to a complete halt.[48]

In the early 1840s the condition of agricultural labourers in the county remained as bad as it had been in the 1830s. The small improvements in wages made as a result of the Swing Riots had dropped back and average local wages, which had been two shillings and three pence a day in the late 1830s fell to two shillings in the early 1840s.[49]

When Edward Tufnell wrote his annual report in 1842, he had a grim year to reflect on. The winter of 1841 had been the worst for 50 years, the hop crop had almost entirely failed and the autumn had been so wet that nearly all

---

[48] ibid
[49] CKS GHb Acb 3

agricultural work had come to a halt.[50] Nevertheless Tufnell's opinion was that the poor were learning to manage their resources better and that fewer had turned to the ratepayers for help. Strangely, he did believe that the wages in the county were adequate, (one wonders on what evidence), and that since the Poor Law Act the farmers were more likely to keep their men on whatever the weather.

It might be thought that migrating to another part of England where there was more work would be a more appealing option than emigration. However very few families from Kent were assisted to migrate to the north of England to work in factories at this time - less than 50. It seems that the factories held no appeal compared with a new land where they would be able to continue in agriculture.

Tufnell's view was that emigration did not always produce the expected result upon the village the emigrants left behind them.

'Emigration has been carried on from Kent and Sussex to a far greater extent than from any other part of England of equal area, and nothing can be more satisfactory than the results, as far as regards the emigrants themselves who have almost invariably sent home the most cheering accounts of their circumstances, They have chiefly gone to Australia, and the colony seems as pleased with them as they with the colony; but the trivial effect produced on the parishes which they have left is very remarkable and by no means easy to be explained. The small comparative decrease in population and of pauperism,

---

[50] 8th annual report of Poor Law Commissioners

which a considerable efflux of emigrants produces, and the rapidity with which a parish, whose numbers have thus been diminished appears to return to its former populous state, is almost incredible; but I find that such has always been the result of emigration in former periods from this district, and I will adduce some proof..'[51]

The facts seemed to support his view, for by 1835 there were again about 60 able-bodied men on the parish relief in Benenden with 360 wives and children, and 12 single able-bodied men. So within seven or eight years after the emigration, the parish appeared to have reverted to its old state of pauperism. On the other hand the Commissioners' 11th annual report contained a letter to them from Thomas Law Hodges which showed that in 1835 there were actually only 37 able bodied men with families in Benenden who were receiving relief, (they were in work but receiving relief to supplement their income because of large families), and that the condition of those remaining was good. By 1842 no less than 341 people had left Benenden for the colonies and rates had decreased over the years. Parish records show that groups left the parish in 1837, 1838, 1840 and 1844.

Hodges wrote *'I believe from no other parish has emigration proceeded with reference to its population to a greater degree than from the parish in which I live, nor anywhere have its effects on the rates been more carefully watched and recorded. The rate payers united in seeing all the advantages.'*

Hodges continued

---

[51] ibid

'I am far from considering the condition of the labourers, even in this parish, as being as comfortable as it ought to be and as I well remember it to have formerly been; but I have the strongest conviction that their condition would not have been what it is now..had not so many of their fellow-labourers possessed the good sense and the spirit to avail themselves of the opportunities offered them of seeking independence among their countrymen who are settled in other parts of the world.'

But Tufnell, the assistant poor law commissioner for Kent and Sussex, had concluded, from the example of Benenden and other parishes, that it was 'entirely hopeless to attempt to benefit the country by any general system of emigration'. He believed this because he thought so many people would need to go in order to make a big difference, and that such a number could not support themselves in the colonies. He considered that some couples even rushed into marriage to qualify for emigration, their cottages instantly taken by couples who had been waiting for accommodation in order to marry.

Notwithstanding his views, whenever Tufnell was consulted about emigration by Boards of Guardians he always encouraged it, believing that both the emigrants and the colonies gained, even if he thought that it did little to decrease the surplus population or save on the poor rates.

When the Poor Law Commissioners wrote their 9th annual report in 1843 they could report that assisted emigration in the previous year had been more extensive than for some years previously.[52] Over a thousand people

---

[52] 9th annual report of the Poor Law Commissioners

had gone, from England and Wales, three quarters of them to Canada.

The Poor Law Commissioners' enthusiasm for emigration seems to have been based more on the good it would do to the parishes they left, than the good it might do the emigrants. They were far less concerned to choose skilled young workers as emigrants than were the Colonial Office or the New Zealand Company as we shall see. In fact the Commissioners were keen to get rid of those who were a burden on the rates although these people would be less likely to make a go of it abroad.

For Kent the numbers who were assisted to emigrate annually by Poor Law procedures were small, often around the 300 mark from the mid 1830s to mid 1840s. Nevertheless Kent, Somerset and Sussex provided the highest numbers. During the years 1836 to 1846 1400 people a year were assisted to emigrate from England and Wales under the auspices of the Commissioners.[53] Yet these numbers never formed more than a small proportion of the total at a time when 18,000 people a year were emigrating.

In the 1850s there were proposals for pauper children without families to emigrate alone and this became a common procedure later in the century. However by the 1850s the numbers being assisted to emigrate through the Commissioners had become very low. The British

---

[53] Johnson S, A history of emigration from the United Kingdom to North America, (1923)

economy was thriving, the Great Exhibition opened in 1851 and the number of emigrants dropped.

England disappears from view. [Illustrated London News 19 July 1852]

Getting there

We seek a land across the sea
Where bread is plenty and men are free
The sails are set, the breezes swell
England, our country, farewell, farewell!
[Sep 13 1873 Illustrated London News]

Emigrants went through a time of great activity as they prepared to leave their homes and villages. There were the clothes to make and the few items of furniture to try to sell. Then the distress and sadness of saying goodbye to loved ones in the knowledge that their only future contact would be by letter, if they were literate. For many this would have been a desperately sad time whilst others would have been filled with hope and some excitement. Going with a group of relatives and friends as most of the assisted emigrants did, must have helped morale enormously and given them courage as they launched themselves into the unknown. The majority were also upheld by a strong Christian faith and a belief that they would be able to advance the fortunes of their families in their new land.

Some would have had their faith strengthened by special prayers and services held for them as departure drew near. The vicar of East Farleigh, the Rev. John Jebb, preached a special sermon in the church on the Sunday before eight families set off for Australia. It was April 1838, the week before Easter and he offered communion which was not then given every Sunday so that the parishioners could share communion together for one last time.[54] Those leaving were told that they would be upheld by the prayers of their fellow worshippers and reminded that it was unlikely that they would all be together again before judgement day when their souls would be before God. Jebb drew comparisons between the great preparations they had been making to travel to Australia and those they should also make for their eternal souls. They were enjoined to keep their faith in the new country with regular family prayers and bring up their children in the love of God. The service finished with the vicar blessing the emigrants.

An article in the Illustrated London News written in 1844 vividly describes a cheerful group of emigrant villagers making their way to the Deptford docks:

'There were two covered hay-wagons…the women and children, with but few exceptions, occupied the conveyances, which were loaded with packages, bundles and boxes; a few of the more elderly females walked on the pathway by the side of their husbands and sons; the younger men trudging it with seeming glee, and carrying various articles we conjecture for immediate use…the leafless trees and hedges-the miry road, with long serpentine wheel tracks; the yellow wagons with their inanimate and living freight, covered with light canvas; the women habited in blue or red cloaks, men in their frocks blending in colour with the many hues of the bundles; and above all, the object of their journey was well calculated to excite human sympathy. Yet no one appeared sad or sorrowful, on the contrary, all seemed to be cheerful; and their clean and

---

[54] Jebb, J, A sermon preached in the parish church of East Farleigh on the Sunday before Easter, April 8th 1838 on the occasion of the approaching migration of eight families from that parish to Australia.

decent appearance bore witness to the propriety of their general habits' [55]

No doubt some did set off filled with optimism but the unpleasant realities of shipboard life would soon have depressed their spirits. For most of us these days it is difficult to imagine spending months at sea in poor conditions and indeed it is difficult to imagine how unpleasant the conditions on board 19th century emigrant sailing ships were. The vessels were small, especially during the first half of the century. The passengers were cooped up in steerage quarters for weeks or months at a time at very close quarters to strangers as well as to family. There would be much discomfort, little privacy, and the danger of falling prey to infectious diseases especially for babies and children. Then there would be the daily embarrassment of trying to get dressed and washed without being observed.

There were three decks; the upper or quarter deck from which orders were given and where the officers and cabin passengers had their quarters, the main deck and the between deck which consisted of the sleeping compartments for the emigrants. Here the air was stale and everything was soon damp. The emigrants cooked their food on the main deck, the facilities for this often consisted only of a half barrel lined with bricks and topped with iron bars to form a grill where the women had to take their turn at cooking their families' rations. Clothes were washed on the main deck, tubs were supplied and drying lines rigged up. Heavy baggage was

---

[55] Illustrated London News 1844 Dec 21

stowed in the lowest part of the hold with the wood for fuel. The steerage where the emigrants slept had little headroom and two layers of berths ran round the sides. Sanitation was primitive and every group of emigrants were advised to take bottles of vinegar to use as disinfectant. It is small wonder that some passengers died during such crossings.

Only 5 ½ feet had to be provided between decks and some of that space was taken up by supporting beams. Again it is the Illustrated London News that provides a description of the conditions below deck on an emigrant ship preparing to leave the London docks in the 1840s. The reporter went below deck:

'We went down into the hold, which was fitted up with berths, and straw mattresses, upon these,..we saw many of the emigrants, waiting wearily for the appointed hour that was fixed for sailing. It made the heart sicken to picture that hold, when with the hatches battened down and the vessel driving through a storm.' [56]

The voyage to Australia and New Zealand took months and during the 1820s and 1830s the voyage to Canada could also last for months depending on the weather. This was a time of limbo for the emigrants who had left their known world behind and had yet to begin their new lives. The length of the voyage would reinforce their belief that they were going to a place unimaginably far from home. For those going to Australia or New Zealand every kind of weather would be encountered. Certainly

---

[56] Illustrated London News 1848 Jul 29

there were dangers in these early years; shipwrecks occurred in which all the passengers died, although a more likely death was by illness caught on board ship.

The route across the Atlantic to America was only a quarter of the distance to Australia but in the early decades of the 19th century was more dangerous since it was not regulated by the government. There were many ships wrecked and lives lost during the 1830s. The vessels on the Atlantic route were over-crowded and some in poor repair. The poor were often packed into converted wooden cargo ships that made the return crossing to Quebec.

There had been a number of laws passed to improve conditions on emigrant ships over the years. The Passenger Acts of 1823 and 1825 brought in some controls; every ship was to have a qualified doctor and must only leave from recognised ports. It was found that these acts restricted ship owners too much and they were repealed in 1827. For the next six months there was no legislation to protect passengers and there were many abuses of overcrowding. So a new Act was passed in 1828, a further one followed in 1835, their aim was better conditions for the emigrants. But still conditions remained poor into the 1840s with some vessels being inadequately examined before setting off, not enough water carried, and incapable surgeons employed. There was a severe outbreak of cholera in Europe in 1832 and the Canadian authorities tried to prevent its spread there by setting up a quarantine station in the St Lawrence estuary where all ships were stopped and inspected. However epidemics of cholera and typhoid spread rapidly through crowded ships and thousands died in

Montreal and Quebec. In 1847 typhus was the threat, and again many emigrants brought the infection with them and died on the voyage.

Once out at sea the emigrants were reliant on the goodwill and capabilities of the captain, surgeon and crew. There were some well run ships with thoughtful captains and doctors who did all they could for those in their charge; there were also negligent unkind ones where the passengers suffered greatly.

On board ship [Illustrated London News Aug 17 1850]

On every emigrant ship a surgeon-superintendent was in charge of the welfare of passengers. It is hard to underestimate the importance of these doctors to the success of the voyage. They were required to keep a log of the voyage noting illnesses that occurred and treatments given to the patients. It was also their responsibility to supervise the giving out of the food rations and they were able to stop rations as a punishment, if for example a man had hit his wife or been abusive to the captain. The surgeons also oversaw the cleaning of the emigrants' quarters which had to be washed down, regularly swept and the beds aired. The passengers were allowed on deck as frequently as possible to take the air. To maintain morality on board, sleeping quarters for men and women were as far away from each other as possible and no drinking or gambling was allowed.

The barque *Westminster* sailed for Sydney from Gravesend in March 1838; all the 251 emigrants on board came from Kent. The surgeon was Dr James Lawrence a conscientious man who wrote that *'The grand objects kept steadily in view during the whole voyage were, the improvement of their minds.'* He was also meticulous in trying to keep the emigrants healthy, every day he inspected the people and the ship, paying great attention to cleanliness, ventilation and food. The berths and decks were scraped and rubbed and disinfected with chloride of lime. The lower deck was washed several times and there was always plenty of soap and water for personal washing. In spite of his care ten died on the voyage, nine of these were under two years old and the tenth, a child of nine died of diarrhoea when they had set sail.

Records show that life at sea was highly organised with many ships having a makeshift school for the children on deck. John Morgan, one of the *Westminster* emigrants had seven other 'teachers' working under his direction to teach the children reading, writing and arithmetic. They were taught the catechism and the surgeon had made sure he was well equipped with books. He described John Morgan as an 'indefatigable teacher.' The children attended school for four hours a day, weather permitting, once they had recovered from their seasickness. The surgeon also had a good supply of books on travel, history and geography to lend to the adults, as well as Bibles and religious texts. Of the 251 emigrants on board over 100 were children and 60 of these were old enough to be educated. There were a number of musical passengers too, with their instruments, whose playing raised everyone's spirits. Wise, experienced surgeons encouraged as many organised activities as possible to avoid the destructive effects of boredom on a crowded vessel.

Emigration vessel – between decks [The Illustrated London News May 10ᵗʰ 1851]

The voyage of the *Westminster* lasted three months and three days. One of the families on board was that of William Thomas a carpenter from the village of Aldington and his wife Sarah. What a contrast between the old life and the new; William found work the day after landing at a good rate of pay.[57]

The *Cornwall*, an East Indiaman, left Deptford for Sydney on 5th May 1839 towed by two steamboats. Arriving at Gravesend on the 7th she received 387 Kentish emigrants on board; 150 men, 94 women and 153 children under 15. Many of the emigrants came in groups from Rolvenden, Benenden, Hythe, Sandhurst, Woodchurch and Romney, so they had the company of friends and neighbours. A journal of the voyage was kept by Thomas Hatfull who assisted the surgeon Dr King. The original and that of the surgeon's report, are in the Library of New South Wales, but transcripts are held at the Centre for Kentish Studies.[58] Hatfull largely confined himself to noting the weather and the ship's position but occasionally his journal is much more informative. He records the cheerfulness of the emigrants in the first weeks as they held a dance every evening on deck. Dr King's report shows that this continued, the emigrants were after all overwhelmingly young: *'There was singing and dancing on deck every lawful day.'* That must have helped enormously to keep everyone well and in good spirits.

School was set up and held regularly for 40 to 60 children. Church service was held every Sunday on deck or below if the weather was poor.

---

[57] Information from Colleen Fisher one of William's descendants
[58] CKS TR3533 Z1, 2

Dancing on deck [Illustrated London News 6 July 1850]

Those who were able, wrote letters or diaries, sewed or played cards; it all passed the time and alleviated the boredom. New and lasting friendships were made amongst the emigrants but there were also bitter quarrels and occasional fights.

Dr King established good routines for the emigrants whereby they washed themselves every morning and there were two clothes washing days each week. Once a week the emigrants' boxes were opened on deck for airing. If it was dry the decks were cleaned every morning. In spite of this care for hygiene the first death on board occurred on the 29th May when thirteen month old Harriet Harding died, a mere three weeks into the voyage.

This being the first burial at sea Hatfull had assisted with, he recorded the details: *'30th May I assisted the sail maker to enrol the body in a blanket at sunset, it was covered with the flag and ballast attached to the feet.'* The service was read and the little body slid over the side. That same day, with Dr King laid up ill himself, Hatfull had been called below to see a child, nine year old Jane Haines who had been suffering for some time with inflammation of the lungs; she died within minutes. On the 17th of June five children died within 24 hours and the following day an alarmed Dr King was well enough to return to duty. He ordered all bags and boxes carried on deck and exposed to the air. Samuel Britcher one of the emigrants refused to obey and defied the doctor. Britcher told the doctor that he, Dr King, was their servant and that he would report him to the government. Of course Dr King reported Britcher to the captain who had him carried up on deck for his insolence, then Dr King cut his rations causing one or two of the other men to object.

You can imagine how the spirits of the emigrants soared as at last they caught sight of their new homeland. The voyage had not been a disaster from the medical point of view according to the standards prevalent at the time. There had been 18 deaths from fever, diarrhoea, rubella and scarlet fever. No one had been ill in bed for the last six weeks and five babies had been born during the passage.

All was bustle on board as a most important visitor was expected:

'At daylight all hands busily employed cleaning ship and making preparations to receive Governor Sir George Gipps and during morning were visited by a number of gentlemen to select servants for their Estates. One came to look for a wife. About noon I went on shore and strolled into the domain or Government Garden, the scenery, and flowers very beautiful. At 2pm His Excellency the Governor came on board and after looking round expressed himself highly pleased both with the ships accommodation and the condition of the emigrants.'

We do not know what Hatfull thought of the man who came to choose a wife, nor whether this was a common event. Did he find a willing woman? If only Hatfull had added a comment.

The following day the emigrants landed and Hatfull went to Sydney Hospital to be given a tour by the principal surgeon. On the 5th he visited the Customs House and the Barracks where the emigrants were boarded and lodged free for 14 days, by the end of which time it was expected that all would have found work.

In 1841, the *London* which had already sailed to New Zealand the previous year and was a large ship of 700 tons set sail again. On this occasion Dr Turnbull was the surgeon on board and 55 emigrant couples, 15 single men, 13 single women, 95 children and 26 babies were on board. In addition there were seven cabin passengers and 17 intermediate who had paid for better quarters. Fifteen emigrants died, ten under two years old, three aged two and two adults. They died of dysentery, diarrhoea, bronchitis and pneumonia. Diarrhoea was always a threat with the passengers closely packed, insufficient facilities to keep clean, and most emigrant ships carrying many children who were of course, more susceptible. Then there was the lack of effective medicines at the time. The medical comforts that the surgeons had available as well as their medicine chest, were brandy, wine, porter, (mostly for mothers who were breastfeeding), rice, limejuice, and mutton.

The actual route taken to Australia changed over time. The sailing ships in the first half of the 19th century took a route which was over 13,000 nautical miles to Sydney and New Zealand an extra 1,200 miles. The route was to Tenerife, the Cape Verde islands, and down to Cape Town, then came the long crossing of the southern Indian Ocean. The route was shortened in the 1850s to go well south of Cape Town, and the average time taken fell to 80 days. The new route meant a great range of climatic conditions for those on board. Going south from England was pleasant but as ships neared the equator and entered the doldrums the heat became oppressive. There they could remain for two or three weeks waiting for the favourable wind. As they sailed south the air would grow colder and colder and snow frost and ice were encountered in the southern Indian Ocean beyond Cape Town.

The advent of steam ships transformed emigrants' experiences of the voyage to their new home. The first steam ship crossed the Atlantic in 1833, taking just thirty days. The Cunard Company was founded in 1840 with four vessels, although of necessity emigrants continued to use the cheaper sailing ships none of which had originally been built for passengers. Nevertheless steam ships gradually ousted sail, bringing vastly improved conditions. Ships sailed at the stated time instead of being reliant on weather conditions. Death rates on board ship fell rapidly. Steam ships reduced the five-month voyage to Australia to five weeks. In the 1860s the average passage by steamer to Canada took thirteen days from Liverpool. In 1863 45% of emigrants had arrived in Canada by steamship. By 1870 they all came by steam.[59] No longer did emigrants feel that they would never be able to return to Britain and in fact many did return.

In 1840 the Colonial and Land and Emigration Commissioners set out to improve the Passenger Acts and to ensure a proper regulation of numbers carried in ships. They were conscientious and brought about real improvements so that death rates on ships fell steadily.[60] The commissioners also drew up detailed regulations for the life of the passengers on board. They were to get up at 7a.m., breakfast between 8 and 9, dinner at 1p.m., supper at 6p.m. They were to be in bed by ten. When they got up in the morning they were to roll up their beds, sweep the decks and throw the dirt overboard. There would be a rota of sweepers taken from males over 14; their tasks included cleaning the decks thoroughly after breakfast. Every ship was to have a hospital. Beds were to be aired and shaken on deck at least twice a week. Two days a week were for washing clothes but none were to be washed or dried between decks. Cooking pans and coppers would be cleaned every day.

Smoking was not allowed between decks and any fighting, swearing or gambling was to be stopped

[59] Kohli M, The golden bridge – young immigrants to Canada 1833-1939
[60] Johnson S, A history of emigration

immediately. Obviously a disciplined existence was essential in the close confinement of a ship.

After 1834 when the Poor Law Commissioners had standardised arrangements for assisted emigration, agreements were always signed between the union guardians and the shipbrokers. A typical one was that drawn up in 1852 between the guardians of the Blean Union and John Bonus a London shipbroker.[61] Funds had been raised for nine of the poor from Herne to go to Canada. Bonus agreed to take them on the ship the *Leonard Dobbin* from the Port of London to Quebec. He took no money from them; he fed them, he gave them medical attendance, wooden bowls, 10 cubic feet for luggage and sleeping room not less than six feet long and 18 inches wide and giving each adult £1 on landing and each child ten shillings. The guardians agreed to pay Bonus £6-10 shillings per person.

Provisions for a man were laid down

Per day	Per week
½ lb meat except Friday when 1lb rice	*8 oz sugar*
½ lb bread	*1 ¾ oz tea*
1lb potatoes	*½ lb cheese*
½ lb flour	*1pt oatmeal*
3 qts water	*6 oz suet*
	½ pt vinegar
	½ lb split peas

---

[61] CKS G/BLAW7

Women were entitled to slightly less. This diet varied somewhat over the years.

Medical attendance had to be provided on board and 'wine and medical comforts' for those who fell ill. The ten cubic feet for luggage was also part of the standard contract as was the sleeping space. It was also agreed that no alcohol be sold to the emigrants on board ship.

'Medical comforts' consisted of preserved meats and soup, scotch barley and bottles of port used to supplement the diet and tempt the palate of those who became ill.

The length of the voyage to Australia or New Zealand in 1852 was such, at around four months, that the emigration authorities laid down in the regulations that they must all be kitted out with a great deal of clothing.[62] The clothing was inspected at the port before embarkation and they could be turned back if they lacked the required amount.

For Men	For women
6 shirts	6 shifts
6 pair stockings	2 flannel petticoats
2 pair shoes	2 pair shoes
2 complete suits exterior clothing	2 gowns

There was also the fact that during the voyage they would pass through both periods of very hot and

---

[62] NA MH19/22

extremely cold weather. To cut down infection emigrants also had to bring their own bedding.

By the 1870s emigrant voyages were no longer dangerous and it had become realistic to imagine being able to return to England if you wanted to, once you had saved enough money, and to know you could arrive back there fit and healthy. But the younger newly arrived émigrés were not likely to be thinking such thoughts as they prepared to leave the cramped conditions of their ship and make their way in this new world. The future, like the country, was a vast unknown. It would have seemed intimidating to some, and they must have paused to look back with something like longing at the ship – their last link with their old lives in Kent.

Emigration to Canada after 1835

'Some are respectable and some we shall be glad to get rid of'

Assisted emigration to Canada was not new. After the Napoleonic Wars discharged men mostly from Highland regiments were given grants of land there if they would emigrate. Then between 1819 and 1827 the British government occasionally voted small sums for paupers' passages to Canada. In 1826 hundreds of thousands of acres of Canadian land were sold by the government to the new Canada Company for a nominal price on the understanding that the company would take out emigrants and develop the area.

Emigrating to Canada or America was always more popular than going to Australia or New Zealand, once they became options, because the shorter distance made it so much cheaper to get there. When assisted passages to Canada became available, that became the chosen route for many poor people some of whom always intended to make America their eventual destination.

Between 1825 and 1846 over 600,000 emigrants landed at Canadian ports. For those who arrived without money to take them further than Quebec, the early experience of the colony was bleak. They were thrown together in the towns where there were too many workers and not enough jobs.

Emigration to Canada could only be undertaken during a portion of the year

69

'as the state of the River St Lawrence during the winter months prevents the access of emigrant ships; and as the average length of voyage is about 6 weeks, and the earliest period of arrival at Quebec is about March.'[63]

The Canadian government provided some help for destitute immigrants who needed to get transport to the interior where they could find work.

Taking the decision to emigrate and leave your entire known world behind could never have been done easily, it was after all the most far reaching decision of a life time, and so inevitably, there were many cases of minds being made up to go and then changed again. In some instances whole groups from a parish planned to leave and then backed out. In 1835 Stockbury was such a place, here, two families and five single young men; a total of 21 parishioners wished to emigrate to Canada with the assistance of the parish. Then as the vicar, Rev David Twopeny wrote in the vestry book: *'The whole of the above persons afterwards refused to go by which they occasioned the parish great trouble and expense.'*[64]

In May Jesse Standen had asked to emigrate to Canada with his wife and eight children if the parish would pay their passage and give them the totally unrealistic sum of £50 on landing. The parish offered £30 on landing which the Standens considered but ultimately turned down. James Burr his wife and four children would go too. He had asked the parish for £30 on landing and was offered £18. He declined. George Kitney, a single man asked for

---

[63] 8th annual report of Poor Law Commissioners 1842
[64] CKS P348 / 8 /1

£5 on landing and was offered £3. He turned it down. This group clearly felt that in order to launch into the unknown they required sufficient money to survive if all did not go well but the sums they were offered were very generous.

Meanwhile the parish finances were still being stretched to their limits in the attempt to support the poor. In July the weekly pay given by the parish for children had to be reduced from 1s 3d to one shilling to make the money go further. So desperate were the Stockbury parish finances that in April 1836 a new list of the cottages in the parish was produced to find out whether anyone else could be called upon to pay poor rate. It was agreed that only the wheelwright could.

A year later a very large group of parishioners, some the same ones as before, decided they would like to emigrate This group was made up of Thomas and Amy Gransden, in their twenties with two children, Stephen and Frances Lambkin also in their twenties with two young children, two young couples in their twenties with no children, George and Sarah Standen and William and Mary Beecham, and also George and Ann Mills in their thirties with five children. James and Hannah Burr in their thirties with four children, Richard and Rebecca Lambkin also in their thirties with seven children, William and Jane Syflet also in their thirties but with no children and the Lambkin brothers' parents, Leonard and Elizabeth, in their sixties were also to go. Two young single men William Gibbs and Moses Whitehead made up this large group.

The wife of Richard Whitehead also applied to be sent out with six children to her husband who had been transported for life to Van Diemens Land (now Tasmania). The parish decided to enquire whether it was permitted to send her out. Richard Whitehead had appeared at the summer assizes at Maidstone in 1833 and been sentenced to transportation for life. His offence was to have slashed 500 hop bines on the grounds of Mr Dawson the Stockbury overseer who had had him imprisoned for his involvement in the Swing Riots. Richard was held on board the *Retribution* hulk at Sheerness in July and embarked for Australia in August. It is not known for sure whether his wife was successful in her application but she may well have been as her presence is not recorded in the Stockbury village census of 1841.

And so it was that April 1837 found the Rev Twopeny, writing to the Poor Law Commissioners about this large number of his parishioners who were now set upon emigrating. They knew of a place which sounded promising- New Whitby, in the Newcastle district of Upper Canada. Most emigrants at this date set off for the unknown without a specific place to live in mind, but they knew a villager who had settled there previously and done well. Such contacts were enormously influential in enabling people to make the decision to leave England behind. There were 39 people including children in the group. Rev. Twopeny explained the local situation:

'Before the new poor law this was one of the most pauperised and worst conducted areas. There was a mob in winter 1830-1 and a stack burnt and subsequently a great part of a hop

garden destroyed out of revenge to an overseer for doing his duty, for which offence a man was apprehended and transported for life. The population is about 700, and is more than the parish can employ.

Last year passages were engaged and emigration agreed but at last moment all refused to go. Now they really desire to and have connections at New Whitby and more would go next year. Some are respectable and <u>some we shall be glad to be rid of.</u>' [65]

In spite of the Rev. Twopeny's underlining how undesirable some of the would-be emigrants were, the Commissioners gave their sanction.

The sending of so many people naturally involved a large expenditure. The passage cost £5 per adult and £2-10 per child. Then there was money to be given on landing £1 per adult and 6s 8d for each child. Clothing was to be provided at a cost of £5 for a large family and £1/6/8 a small one. The total expenses of the journey were £3 to Gravesend, steam boat to London £2/1/8, passage to Montreal £143, on to New Whitby £55. The parish overseer needed to go to London to see them off which cost a further £5. So the grand total was £250, which the Stockbury ratepayers borrowed.

The group did indeed reach New Whitby, (now Whitby), and settle there. [66] New Whitby then was a small town with a population of 2,600. Directories of the town during the 1840s and 1850s show a number of the heads of household engaged in farming various lots in the east of

---

[65] NA MH12 5134
[66] Thanks to Brian Winter archivist of Whitby.

the township. William Gibbs, Stephen and Leonard Lambkin, Thomas Gransden and James Burr were all there.

In 1835 the parish of Ospringe in the Faversham Union raised £160 in order to send a large group to Canada. The accounts were carefully kept listing the price of the passage, provisions and landing money for each of the 16 people, with a similar outlay to the Stockbury group. William Foster his wife Sarah and their six children had their fares paid by the Ospringe vestry. The family had been a drain on the parish's finances for years.[67] William Foster suffered frequent ill-health but did occasional work for the parish at a shilling a day, he had also been caught poaching. All in all the parish rate payers would be glad to see the back of them.

A further long list was written into the account book of those 'desirous of emigrating', to wait until funds allowed. By 1843 the parish were able, to send a further group, of eight people, to Quebec on the ship the *Resource*. One of those who embarked at Gravesend was Sarah Wellard an 18 year old inmate of the workhouse.

There are many examples from parishes all over Kent of emigration to Canada after 1835. In 1836 George Spain and his family of wife and five children were assisted by

---

[67] Stevens J, Faversham's reluctant exiles

Preston-next-Wingham parish to go to Mansfield (in Canada), where they had relations who had already been helped to settle there by the Thanet union.[68]

In Saltwood two groups of villagers were ready to go to different destinations, Quebec and New York.[69] In the event only the Johnson family went to New York and the remainder of the 34 embarked for Canada. The parish raised £250 by loan and this covered the cost. What each family had cost the parish in the year before they sailed was noted: the Smeed and Johnson families over £6 each, the Webbs over £10, the Hams over a £1 and the Wards over £2. The young single men had cost over £1 each. In all over £40 had been spent to sustain the group that year and the rate payers could feel confident that it would not take many years to recoup their investment in sending then abroad.

In Bethersden that year a different way of raising the necessary funds was used. A voluntary rate was raised to allow Celia Evenden a widow to emigrate to America with her four children.[70] The parish repeated the exercise in 1839 when another voluntary rate raised the money for Phoebe Price and her seven children to go to America.

A party of young labourers from Sutton Valence some with wives and families, left for Quebec in 1840 aided by money raised by parish rate, probably accompanied by a group from the nearby village of Leeds. In the same year eight adults and 22 children departed from

[68] CCA U3 / 245 / 16 / 94
[69] CCA U3 / 147 / 8 / 1
[70] CKS U24 A31

Headcorn for Montreal along with 25 from Chart Sutton. Each adult was given £1 to start them off in their new life. Contact was made with Carter and Bonus, London ship owners and emigration agents, to convey the families leaving in April on the ship *Urania*. Carter and Bonus' advertisements stated that they could ease the burden on parishes by ridding them forever of dependant families for the cost of 'one year's maintenance'.[71]

The following year the parish of Headcorn raised £100 for further emigration, and 27 parishioners sailed for Canada on the *Prince George* in April 1842. The ratepayers of Headcorn continued to borrow money to send their poverty stricken neighbours to the colonies in 1843.

Goudhurst had raised considerable sums for emigration in 1839, 1840 and 1841. In 1842 a letter arrived at the Cranbrook Union workhouse from Thomas Webb, uncle of Sophia and Charles Tipping who were inmates and came from Goudhurst. Thomas Webb asked if the workhouse guardians would pay the children's passage to Canada where their mother had already gone. He offered to take charge of the children as he was emigrating himself. In May he attended the board of guardians meeting and they consented to his taking the children and paid him £2 towards their fare to Portsmouth and £15 to take them to Toronto where their mother was living.

Regular certificates appear in union guardians' minutes sent from the Poor Law Commissioners regarding the

---

[71] Stevens J, Faversham's reluctant exiles

safe conveyance of emigrants to their destination. They were proof that the contract with Carter and Bonus had been fulfilled and payment was then deducted from the various parish emigration accounts. For example in 1842 the emigrants from Hawkhurst to Montreal arrived safely on the *Orbit*. Certificates of satisfaction arrived at the Cranbrook Union workhouse from the Poor Law Commissioners on the ships' arrival at Montreal.

And when all these emigrants arrived in Canada there were procedures to be followed and if their health was in question they were assessed by a doctor. A certain Dr Poole was responsible for examining the emigrants who arrived at the quarantine station, Grosse Island Quebec at this time. He wrote to the Secretary of State:

'The poorer class of English paupers sent by parishes were on arrival in many instances entirely without provisions, so much so, that it was necessary to supply them with food immediately from shore, and some of these ships had already received food and water from other vessels with which they had fallen in…This destitution or shortness of provisions, combined with dirt and bad ventilation had invariably produced fevers of a contagious character and occasioned some deaths on the passage…numbers have been admitted to hospital immediately.' [72]

In 1843 the chief agent of the Quebec emigration office, Alexander Buchanon, wrote to the government in London giving his opinion that

---

[72] NA MH19/22

'the object of rate payers seems to be not so much to benefit the emigrants as to obtain the removal of the redundant pauper Labourers of a parish and thereby to reduce the poor rate...'

And indeed this seemed to be the driving force of the Poor Law Commissioners' enthusiasm for emigration. They did not concern themselves with the balance of numbers between the two sexes in the new colonies; from the Cranbrook and Tenterden Unions they sent twice as many single men as single women.[73] They were most likely to send large families and older adults who were a great drain on the poor rates. By contrast the colonisers wanted fit young married couples with health and energy to contribute to the development of their new country.

A letter written in 1834 by a Mr E Harvey of Hythe; a wealthy man with another house in Russell Square London shows the attitude of some rich people to assisted emigration:

'I generally disapprove of sending good labourers out of the country but here it appears are two or three families not of the best character.... As such I should quite concur with the zeal of the parish in carrying their resolution into effect. When the overseer calls I will pay.' [74]

Meanwhile in the Quebec immigration department Alexander Buchanon noted that there were thousands of emigrants who were doing well but also large numbers who remained in the same extreme poverty that they had

---

[73] Wojciechowska-Kibble, B, Journal of Kent History 1980 vol 10 no11.
[74] CKS U47 / 18 / E5

suffered in Britain. He had a sympathy for these poor newcomers and wrote in 1843:

'It is the duty of those directing the arrangements of future emigration to place the immigrants in a situation to be enabled with certainty to take advantage of the opening for industry... or at least secure them from distress or destitution.'

Weekly communications were sent between Canadian officials and the Colonial Office in London so that a close eye could be kept on the situation. Matters appeared to improve for later in 1843 Mr Buchanon reported that the *Amazon* arrived from London with passengers including 58 assisted by the Poor Law Commissioners; all received their £1 landing money and were sent on to Montreal.

A typical weekly report from London to Quebec in 1844 read:

'The families (48) in the Arcturus are paupers sent out by their parishes under the superintendence of the Poor Law Commission, they all received sufficient means to carry them to their destination.'[75]

The chief agent of the emigration office at Quebec replied mentioning 'The comfortable condition in which these emigrants land here'. However he felt that the £1 landing money was seldom enough to take them far into the interior where they needed to go to find work.

---

[75] NA MH 19 / 22

Every enticement was offered to make working people want to emigrate to Canada

Assisted emigration to Canada continued into the 1870s and beyond and advertisements such as the foregoing of 1875 from the Kent and Sussex Times, shows a great shortage of labourers. Considerable free grants of land were being offered and the passage by steam ship only took ten days by that time.

By the 1880s sending orphans to Canada was a well-established idea for the poor law unions. This is another subject in itself, but here is just one case from thousands which occurred. A touching letter arrived at the Blean union workhouse in June 1892 from Halifax, Nova Scotia. It was addressed to the guardians and requested help in paying for the writer's brother and sister to go and live with him.

'We are Orphans and was brought up in the Blean Union workhouse until I became old enough to earn my own living when I was apprenticed and owing to ill treatment on the part of my Master I absconded before I served my time and went to live at Wallington Surrey where after being out of work for a long time I made an application to the Croyden Guardians to assist me in emigrating to this country which after due consideration they voted me £5 which I understand came from the Government grant voted annually for assisting emigration. Since I have been in this country I ordered my brother and sister discharged as inmates of the Blean Union and paid their maintenance ever since it is a great strain on my purse..and I can't continue..but if they were here they could be with me..I ask you for £10'.[76]

---

[76] CKS G/ BL AW 7

Edwin Newing the writer, was an assistant station master on the railway. His brother and sister were boarded with a family at Herne Bay. It was decided that they should be allowed to go. The shipping agents wrote in October 1892, that the two orphan children Nathaniel and Charlotte Newing aged 15 and 13, in the workhouse school, could go from Liverpool to Halifax on the *Carthaginian* from Liverpool.

As time went on emigration schemes for poor children were organised by Dr Barnardo's and the Catholic Emigration Society with the poor law unions. The original idea was to give the children new opportunities, but in fact many children virtually became slave labour on Canadian farms. After early complaints, a system of visiting was introduced using agents of the Emigration Society in Canada. Written reports were posted back to England to the unions.[77] This scandal continued well into the 20th century and reflects the 'out of sight out of mind' attitude of many of those in authority. The financial incentive to relieve the pressure on the rates took precedence over the sense of responsibility for the future safety and well being of even the youngest of the emigrants who had left their charge.

---

[77] Weller M, Bygone Kent vol 16, Children in late Victorian Kent

To Australia

'Many parishes have availed themselves of this opportunity of relieving themselves of some of their surplus population.'

Poor Law Commissioners Report 1843

Emigration to Australia differed from that to Canada in that it originated entirely with the government, using funds from the sale of public lands.

In 1830 it was still the case that more convicts than free settlers were arriving in Australia; the last convict ship would not arrive in Sydney until 1840 and in Van Diemens Land not until 1853.

By 1830 the free settlers needed more labourers from Britain but the fare was too expensive for many to manage. The reformer Edward Wakefield's idea that labourers' fares could be paid to Australia from the proceeds of selling land there, was adopted, so that instead of land being granted to settlers it would be sold. So in 1831 an Emigration Commission was set up to oversee the process of parish supported emigration using the profits from the land sales. Its other purpose was to give information to prospective emigrants. If assisted emigration had not been undertaken for Australia the development of the colony would have been much delayed because of the cost of the passage.

So it was in 1831 that the Colonial Office produced printed information leaflets for parish use to encourage emigration to New South Wales.[78] The cost of the passage was lowered and could be paid for by the parishes: 'For persons desirous of going to New South Wales and Van Diemens Land, passage for people of working classes cost £16 adults, £8 child.' The leaflet explained that workers of all kinds were needed. Labourers would earn £25-£30 a year plus board and lodging whilst artisans with some skills could earn £50 a year. All food was cheap. No single men were required because men so outnumbered women in the colony. Parishes could raise passage money and there would be government officers available at the ports to advise emigrants.

Village labourers were encouraged to emigrate by being given information like this about life in Australia. An interesting example of a more personal approach can be found in two letters which were printed and distributed to labourers:

' particularly to those with large families growing up; to show them the great providence of God in giving them a country where they can receive large wages for their labour and plenty of food. Now, the country they are in, is so thickly inhabited that it is impossible for them to live and bring up their families on their earnings'.[79]

The letters were from Thomas and Lydia Barnes of New South Wales, written in 1838, one to Thomas's uncle a Benenden labourer and one to his mother of Watling Sussex. Barnes had been transported in 1819 for burglary. The letters are very poorly spelt but tell a tale of dramatic

---

[78] CCA U3 / 245 / 16 / 68
[79] CKS U1776 016

rags to riches success. Barnes was paying his workers £25 a year and hoped his letter would persuade more men to come out from Benenden. Now he lived in an eleven roomed house and owned eight horses. In truth Benenden was to have more emigrants than any other parish and this could well have helped towards the total.

In 1837 the post of Agent-General for Emigration was created to be in charge of a team of government agents at British ports. The office of the Agent General was to supply information to prospective emigrants and to supervise shipping arrangements for them, supplying them with food, water, medical supplies, bedding and utensils. Agents were to give priority to farm workers, and craftsmen and were to select the emigrants at meetings which they would advertise in the area.

The most obvious place to find emigrants was amongst the unemployed, so the agents worked closely with the Poor Law Commissioners. It has been said that most of the 13,000 emigrants selected for assisted passage between 1837 and 1840 came from the workhouses of England and Wales.[80] This may be so in other counties, but in Kent most were not inmates. They were however out of work and many had been in and out of the workhouse.

As an article in the Illustrated London News reported:

'It has been generally supposed that the free emigrants are all paupers, glad to escape from the confinement of a union

---

[80] Kitson J., The British to the Antipodes

workhouse; but this is a great mistake. ... the chief portion are cottagers, most of whom have never received parish relief...struggling with numerous difficulties to gain a precarious livelihood and enduring severe ...hardships in the inclement season of winter..' [81]

If we focus on one area of Kent in 1837 we can see how the system worked in practice. The meeting minutes of the guardians of the Cranbrook Union of January 1837 show that a letter was read from the Australian emigration agent, and that months later in December the clerk was asked to prepare a notice to be displayed in the union area calling attention to emigration to New South Wales and how to apply. [82]

Meetings were then held for those interested at Yalding, Cranbrook, Tenterden, Northiam and Battle.

Two ships, the *Amelia Thompson,* and the *Coromandel* were to sail from Gravesend in the spring of 1838, and would be followed by many others. A circular was sent to parishes, setting out the many detailed conditions for the free passages to New South Wales.

The circular explained that there was a great demand in the colony for every kind of married craftsmen from carpenters to wheelwrights. Even more demand existed for farm workers less than 35 years old, or at the most 40, who could have a free passage if they were accompanied by their wives, and were childless. Married people with

---

[81] Illustrated London News Dec 21 1844
[82] CKS G/CR/ AM1

children could be accepted for a free passage if they paid for their children themselves.

For young single men, who were good farm workers, (especially shepherds), the rules were somewhat different. If they were in good health, and of excellent character, they would be allowed a passage for only £5; but other single workers had to pay their own passage of around £21. Single young women, particularly those who had experience of working on dairy farms, or as house servants, were greatly needed in the colony; and only had to contribute a payment of £2 each for their passage. They required a good character reference, and had to go out under the care and protection of a family. Married couples could increase their chances of being accepted if a single woman went with them.

Before 1837 emigrants had been taken to New South Wales in government ships at government expense, however that year, the Bounty System was introduced. It was originally intended to be useful for the settlers who needed specialised labourers, to have them brought out to the colony. The colonial government paid the 'bounty' to the landowners who could choose between say mechanics or farm labourers to come out. The landowner received £30 for a married man and his wife, £10 for a single young man and £15 for a single young woman. In reality the actual 'Bounty orders' were often sold for a fast profit to ship owners who collected emigrants and crammed as many as possible into ships in poor conditions.

The Bounty System was cheaper than using government ships and was preferred by the governor of New South

Wales. The bounty was increased in 1840 when the colony was in great need of more labourers. Emigration on government ships was stopped and numbers coming increased so much that the colony did not have sufficient funds to pay the bounty.

Many emigrants arrived in poor physical condition and had to be supported for weeks after their arrival in New South Wales. Colonists complained about the quality of the workers, whilst colonial officials complained about the cost.

Back in Kent it was explained to the would be émigrés that they were allowed to take a small luggage package into the steerage compartment. All other luggage was stored. The regulations stated that new bedding would be provided for all the passengers; as they were not permitted to take their own bedding on board (except sheets), in case they were dirty or lousy. There were separate sleeping apartments for single male and female steerage passengers, 'and in no case will more than two adults occupy one bed'!

Passengers who were going free were required to send character and health references. These certificates were to be signed by a clergyman, or other respectable inhabitant who knew them well, before any application could be approved. Certificates of age were also required.

Then there was the long list of clothing to last the voyage without which the emigrants would not be allowed on board. Every steerage passenger had to have enough linen and other changes of clothes, for a month's use in a very small box not more than 15 inches square. Only these small boxes were allowed in the sleeping apartments. Once a month during the voyage the larger packages would be brought on deck from the hold, so that everyone could change their dirty clothes for clean ones. Keeping clean under those circumstances must have been impossible. The emigrants had to take their own knife and fork, tablespoon and teaspoon, pewter or tin plate, tin pots, combs, and soap. Taking a Bible was advised.

A doctor's certificate was required as evidence that the emigrants had either had small pox, or been vaccinated against it. Women in advanced pregnancy were advised to delay their family's voyage until after the birth.

All emigrants who travelled out under this Bounty Scheme were told that on arrival, they must go before the board at Sydney to be inspected and would not be entitled to remove their luggage from the ship until they had been examined.

By contrast passengers sufficiently well off to book a cabin paid between £70 and £120, according to the accommodation selected. These passengers travelled under very different conditions being supplied with the best fresh provisions, wines, and beer during the voyage. They brought their own cabin fittings, bedding, and were allowed plenty of luggage space.

Returning to the situation in Kent, the poor summer of 1837 had been followed by a very harsh winter with heavy snow. Many families were destitute and close to starving, and so, in these desperate circumstances many made the decision to try for a new life in New South Wales.

In one such case, the emigration selection officer arrived in Sandhurst, a village in the Cranbrook Union, in April 1838 to see the applicants as required under the new scheme. A letter from a Dr Inches was read out stating that he had received instructions from the Agent General for Emigration to inspect people who wanted to emigrate to New South Wales. He had some leeway in exceeding the 35 year age limit 'where the parties were considered very eligible.' This must have been the case with John and Martha Robards who were accepted when Dr Inches saw them at the workhouse, in spite of their ages; they were then 53 and 47. Thus the emigration selection officer approved a list of people who had already had the sanction of the doctor. This list of names was then put forward for the approval of the parish ratepayers.

On April 27th 1838 a vestry meeting was held at the Swan Inn Sandhurst. Vestry meetings consisted of the churchwardens and overseers and elected representatives of the rate payers of the parish. They decided to raise money to enable John Robards senior, a carpenter, his second wife Martha, James, Henry and Aaron their younger children, John Robards junior, his wife and two children, William Robards 26, his wife Harriet and one child and Stephen Robards 24, his wife Mary and child to emigrate to New South Wales in June.

The Robards were Baptists, all the children having been baptised at the Sandhurst Particular Baptist Chapel.[83]

This large family group were to sail on the *Maitland* from Gravesend. So the Robards had to say farewell to friends and family, homes and loved places knowing they would never return. John's mother, Sarah, was still alive and leaving her must have added to the general sadness. They then all set out together, laden with their clothing and personal effects on the journey to the docks and the ship that awaited them.

The 648 tons *Maitland* was an old wooden frigate. Built in 1810, she measured 125 feet (38 metres), in length and was converted to barque rigging for her voyage to Australia. Nowadays she would be considered very small.

Some livestock was loaded onto the *Maitland* with the 205 adults and 110 children to provide them with fresh food. This group of emigrants were a close knit band of related families, friends and neighbours. There was a large group from Rolvenden and others from neighbouring Kentish parishes and just across the border into Sussex. All embarked on the 21st June and were directed to their cramped quarters below decks. Surgeon-superintendent John Smith, RN embarked on the same day and settled into his more comfortable quarters. Due to the changed selection arrangements he had not met the emigrants before embarkation and had taken no part in their

---

[83] All information on the Robards family with the kind permission of Professor Robards

selection. Hundreds of men, women and children had to settle themselves and their possessions on board in preparation for the long voyage. Dr Smith would have been busy establishing regulations and procedures for health on board and could not have had time to notice that a few of the children were not in the best of health.

Three days after embarkation, on 24th June, the *Maitland* finally sailed under Captain Marshall Baker on a passage that would last 134 days. Only two days after sailing, scarlet fever broke out on ship. Between that date and July 21,st there were over 60 cases of fever. Up to this point the Robards family must have been very worried but thankful to have been spared. What had began as a voyage of hope turned into a nightmare as five adult emigrants, one crew member and 29 children died.

On July 21,st illness did strike the Robards and proceeded to claim the lives of seven of the sixteen. Of the children Henry, Matilda, Ellen and David suffered diarrhoea but went on to recover. Other children in the family also became ill, Aaron had scarletina and died on August 1st aged 6, Ellen was cured of the same illness. Matilda the daughter of John junior and Sophia died aged 18 months of 'marasmus', which Mary Ann recovered from. Marasmus means wasting away. Henry died aged twelve from typhoid on October 1st. On the same day James aged 21 also died of typhoid, James mother Martha died on the same day aged 47. Stephen 23, had died of typhoid in August on the equator and Sophia, John junior's wife, died aged 26 in September. Five other members of the family had appeared on the sick list.[84] Those who were well enough would have attended the funerals on the deck as the body of their brother, daughter, mother or father, was consigned to the ocean.

The morale of the *Maitland* passengers sank extremely low adding to the difficulties inherent in the cramped and crowded conditions on board in which disease had spread rapidly.

Surgeon-superintendent Smith tried to prevent the spread of the disease but met opposition from the parents who didn't want their children removed into the hospital part of the ship. Sometimes he had to force the separation, and this meant that there were fewer sufferers than might otherwise have been the case. Many parents had more than one child ill at a time and were worn out with nursing. To prevent the spread of scarlet fever, all the berths, deck and other fittings were washed with caustic lime and chloride of lime once a week, the bedding was sprinkled, and other articles were frequently cleaned with the chloride of lime.

Infantile fever or marasmus was the next great cause of mortality. It began early in the voyage and continued to the end. Surgeon Smith thought the cause was over feeding the children with the ordinary rations instead of with the arrowroot and sago which was better for them but which the mothers were not keen to give their children. He also had difficulty in persuading the

---

[84] Surgeons journal of the Maitland, information extracted by Professor Robards

emigrants to be as clean as he wished particularly the men, who resisted his instructions about this and about the airing of their bedding.

Married couples accommodation. Bunks on the left, there was little privacy. [Illustrated London News 13 April 1844]

A few of the passengers he found 'extremely insolent and intemperate,' and two married women 'abandoned themselves to vicious habits'. Clearly Smith did not have an easy, confident authority or the personality to get the emigrants on his side. He considered them a lazy bunch, and found only the school to praise. It had been established on board under John Vidler, a Sandhurst man, described by Smith as an able Christian, and the children, who were mostly illiterate, were given basic instruction.

By September the *Maitland* was sailing down the African coast towards the Cape and entered Table Bay on the 19th. There was no communication with the authorities on shore because of the sickness on board. The ship's water supply was replenished during this brief stop.

Soon afterwards the long leg of the journey eastward towards Sydney began

Learning to read on deck [Illustrated London News 20 Jan 1849]

How the spirits of the emigrants must have lifted as the beauties of Sydney Harbour with its wooded hills came in sight. For some though it came too late. By the time they docked John Robards senior had lost his wife and four children and, unsurprisingly, was in a poor state of health himself. He must have been a broken man. He still had his 18 year old daughter Martha with him, his son John however was in no better state, having lost wife and child and having only his three year old daughter Ellen left of his family. Old John's young daughter-in law Mary was now starting her new life as a widow of 21 with a baby.

The *Maitland*, arrived on the 5th of November and a medical inspector was soon on board and placed the ship with her crew and passengers into quarantine. Many of the vessels arriving in the colony at this time brought with them the danger of serious infection, five of 37 immigrant ships which arrived in 1838 had to be quarantined.

The great increase in shipping arrivals and the hazards of the introduction of infectious disease to the colony led Governor Gipps to appoint a Health Officer for the port in December 1838. Vessels from overseas were not permitted to proceed beyond Neutral Bay until visited by the Officer. If the presence of an infectious disease was suspected, all communication with the vessel was forbidden until it was decided whether or not to impose quarantine. The Health Officer was required to make frequent visits to the Quarantine Station.

The North Head of Sydney Harbour was well suited for a Quarantine Station having a deep, safe anchorage for vessels, sloping sandy beaches for ease in landing people and airing cargoes, and fresh water draining from ground above the beach. Four wooden buildings were erected above the beach for the use of healthy immigrants. A hospital was erected on the high ground on the south side of Quarantine Beach in 1838.

The four buildings on the Healthy Ground were wooden, each housing about 25 people. Single men were housed in one end building, single women in the other under the supervision of a matron, whilst married couples and their families were in the two middle buildings. Convalescents were normally segregated in tents on the Sick Ground. Open fireplaces were provided for cooking in the early years. Conditions in the unlined, overcrowded hospital were grim.

The need to quarantine the *Maitland* presented the authorities with problems as it overlapped with that of the *William Roger* and *Palmyra* which had arrived on September 26th and September 27th respectively, and were placed in quarantine. It became necessary to proclaim Little Manly Cove a quarantine station for people landed from the *Maitland*. There were still five diagnosed typhus cases on board and eight or ten cases of intermittent fever.

Beds, bedding and tents were made ready for the *Maitland* emigrants and the quarantine guard went to oversee the 'healthy quarantine station' at Manly Cove, arriving on 9th November. The following morning a total of 225 healthy persons had landed at Manly Cove and there were no further cases of sickness. Some passengers listed as 'healthy' remained on the *Maitland*; no doubt to tend to sick relatives. On November 15th, the sick emigrants were placed in a temporary wooden hospital at Spring Cove.

The Governor's concern is evident in his despatch to Lord Glenelg the secretary of state for the colonies:

'22 November 1838: Sir George Gipps to Lord Glenelg

'I have still further with sorrow to inform your Lordship that we have had occasion also to place in Quarantine the ship Maitland which arrived here on the 6th Inst. with Government Emigrants from Gravesend, after a voyage of 134 days. The Buildings at the Quarantine ground being all occupied by the people of the William Roger, it has been necessary to place the Emigrants by the Maitland under canvas, with exception of those actually sick, for whom a temporary wooden Hospital has been erected. The number of deaths on board the Maitland was 35, Six of whom were adults, and 29 children. The cases of disease entered on the Surgeon's Books were no less than 286; but in this number the same individuals may in some cases have been reckoned more than once. Two women and two children have died since their arrival, and the present number of sick is 13. Scarlet fever was the first disease that broke out among them, but various others afterwards made their appearance.

As soon as these ships are released from Quarantine, I shall institute a strict enquiry, in order to ascertain if possible the cause why sickness has been so much greater in the present year on board Government vessels than those engaged on the same business by private individuals. At present I am utterly unable to account for it; it is suggested that it may be in consequence of the greater number of children embarked in them, or that the Emigrants are in a worse state of health when put on board, or that, being taken from a poorer class of society, they are less prepared with necessaries for the voyage.'

Finally, on 26th November the ship and her crew and passengers (with the exception of those still ill), were released from quarantine. Twenty-six adults from the *William Roger* died in quarantine and 18 children, whilst two adults and three children from the *Maitland* died

98

there. The Governor recorded his displeasure in his despatch to Lord Glenelg.

'20 January 1839: Sir George Gipps to Lord Glenelg

I beg further to report to your Lordship that, considering the disasters which have marked the voyages of both these vessels, the dirty state in which the Emigrants by the Maitland were reported to be on their arrival, and the enormous expenses which have fallen on the Colony by their long detention in Quarantine, I have not judged it proper to issue Gratuities to the Surgeon of the William Roger or to the Surgeon or officers of the Maitland; though, as the Master of the William Roger died in Quarantine, I have not withheld his Gratuity from his Widow.

I have no positive charge of misconduct to prefer against either of the two Surgeons of these two vessels; but the enterprise, in which they engaged, has been signally unfortunate. The loss of their expected Gratuities is also the less heavy upon them, as, in addition to their full pay, they have received the following sums for their services in Quarantine, viz:

The Surgeon of the William Roger £64 The Surgeon of the Maitland £46.'

Gipps was an able governor and was himself a Kentish man.

The Maitland passengers were transferred to the Immigrants' Barracks at the back of Government House where they were put up at government expense while they found accommodation. Immigrants who came under the Bounty System were left to make their own arrangements for accommodation and employment.

New arrivals had to decide whether to sign up with a landowner for steady pay, or take a chance on their own. Prospective employers of emigrants were given notice in the press of emigrants available for hire in various categories. This might occur in the barracks but it could also mean sending some kinds of workers in convoys to distant parts of the colony where they were needed.

John Robards and his surviving family did not remain in Sydney for long. They were living in the settlement of Raymond Terrace by 1840. John junior was a carpenter like his father and there was plenty of work for carpenters in the growing town of Sydney. Nevertheless after a short time he leased a farm in the Raymond Terrace area and it was here that he married Mary the widow of his brother Stephen in 1840. John junior prospered, trying prospecting for gold but then settling to buying and running a hotel.

John Robards senior, John Robards junior and William Robards all engaged with a Mr Lord of Paterson River to the north in the Hunter Valley, doing piece work whilst Mary engaged with a Mr Petty of Sydney as a cook in his hotel for £40 a year. William Gill, a fellow emigrant from the *Maitland*, had also been engaged by Mr Lord and no doubt the Gills and Robards travelled to their new home together. John and a number of other *Maitland* and *Lady Nugent* men entered into a contract with Simeon Lord to lease Leigh Farm for a period 14 years from January 1839. It was an unusual arrangement to share the cost of the lease with nine men including William Gill.

The *Lady Nugent* had also arrived in Sydney in 1838, after the *Maitland*. Many of the emigrants on this vessel were also from Kent and Sussex. Other farming families who settled at Raymond Terrace had arrived on the *Westminster*, in June 1838, and the *Cornwall* in September 1839. The Blanch family from Rolvenden came on the *Westminster*. They were followed by further family members on the *Maitland* and *Cornwall*. All settled in the area of Raymond Terrace. The *Maitland* in particular brought many families to the district - those of George and Mary Wattus, Edward and John Hicks, Uriah Milham, John Clark who lost his wife and child on the voyage and subsequently married Martha Robards, and William and Susannah Gill with their seven children. William's brother Silas Gill had arrived in the colony with his family in July 1837 aboard *Augusta Jessie*. William's eldest daughter Harriet, and her husband Edward King, came on the *Lady Nugent*. The following year yet more members of the Blanch family arrived in the *Cornwall*.

This ship carried James Robards, (brother of John senior), who was also a carpenter, his wife Sarah and children. The oldest child, James junior, was a carpenter too. They settled in Parramatta and then Molong. They worked the goldfields at Ophir and later at the Peak Hill strike then returned to Molong.

Many of the Kentish emigrants were Methodists who founded new chapels in Australia. Most of the early families to settle at Raymond Terrace came from the Sandhurst Methodist Circuit which straddled the Kent/Sussex borders. Two of these families who arrived in Australia on the *Roxburgh Castle* were the Gilberts and the Barnes. This ship left England in January 1839. Unfortunately, in both these families the head of the family died on the way out. The *Roxburgh Castle* in fact suffered a high number of deaths on the voyage, the Gilberts losing Owen, the infant son of their son Thomas and his wife Mary Ann, and after leaving Cape Town, John Gilbert took ill and died and they then suffered another loss in the death of Alice, their youngest child. Samuel Barnes also died at sea. One of the members of the Sandhurst Methodist Circuit was Joseph Nash a Sandhurst man who also arrived in Australia in 1839 with his family of eight children.

Interior of settler's hut in Australia [The Illustrated London News 1849 Mar 17]

The article with it states that the hut was of a type commonly seen in the Bush, constructed of rudely slit logs, and the gaps filled with mud or clay. Joe, the shepherd in the sketch, made the artist warmly welcome with a mutton stew. On his wall was the large poster from the Illustrated London News announcing the Queen's visit to the Nottingham area.

Back in Sandhurst more poor people were making the decision to leave for Australia. In 1841 the guardians of the Cranbrook Union agreed contracts with Carter and Bonus for taking paupers from Hawkhurst and Sandhurst to Sydney. William Catt and his family had left Sandhurst apparently fit and well but had to be disembarked at Cork because the children were suffering from measles. There they remained for six weeks until they were declared well and the next ship could take them. Carter and Bonus wrote to the Cranbrook guardians claiming expenses for having put them up in Ireland and seen they were fed. They claimed the children had had measles when they embarked which the parish officers in Sandhurst disputed.[85]

William and Mary Ann Jeffery came out on the *Lady Nugent*. Jeffrey was born in Brenchley, in 1808, and Mary Ann in neighbouring Goudhurst some two years later. The couple were married in 1828 and had four children before deciding to emigrate in 1838. They were accompanied by only two of their children however, the other two dying in infancy. William was a farm labourer and Mary Ann a farm servant. The couple settled in the Windsor District where they took a pub.

Joseph Dunster and his wife Mary were fellow passengers on that voyage of the *Lady Nugent*. They had left Stone-in-Oxney where Joseph was a shepherd and

---

accompanied by their six children endured the hardships on board. The vibrations of the vessel, the wet bedding from constantly shipping water were hard to endure. The addition of mutton to the passengers' stew from the occasional sheep slaughtered on board, kept up their strength and spirits. The Dunsters settled in the Illawarra where Joseph was engaged to work on a farm at thirty shillings a week. Riches indeed after the miserable wages in Kent! The work was hard for most of the Illawarra was still dense thickets of cedar, cabbage tree palms and creeping vines. No doubt the Dunsters travelled to the Illawarra area by steam ship, overland travel being impractical. The family prospered in farming and contributed to local community life with two of the sons later serving as aldermen.

Another family success story were the Bryant family from Benenden. William and Ann Bryant had married as far back as 1818 and when they set sail on the *Westminster* in 1838 they had a family of seven. Their eldest, a son was 19 years old, and the other six were all girls. William found farm work in Australia at £2 a week and his namesake, young William was employed on a farm for £25 a year, Sarah the eldest daughter, then 17 was employed as a nursemaid. William junior went on to work on the New South Wales railways, eventually becoming the first station master on the Redfern to Parramatta line. He took an active part in civic affairs becoming the first mayor of Waterloo which was then a major suburb of Sydney. He married and had twelve children. His known descendants number over a thousand. By the time of William's death in 1896 he owned two houses and a piece of land. A far cry form his poor childhood in Benenden. William senior and Ann went on to have two further children after they arrived in Australia; John and Alexander. Both of these did well in life. John was appointed station master at Burwood, he was steadily promoted and finished his career as Chief Paymaster in the government railways. Alexander was apprenticed at a flour mill in Sydney, and did so well that he started his own business.[86]

Often, once one member of a family, or even a whole family in a close-knit community had emigrated and sent back good reports about their new life, it provided a spur to others to also consider emigrating. The health risks of the voyage were high, especially for the children, but the rewards were potentially very great. Good, hardworking people were drawn to the challenge and a fear grew up in some places in England that too many good and useful people were being lost. That is why in 1839 the parish vestry of Boxley in the Hollingbourne Union initially borrowed £47 to assist villagers to emigrate but changed its decision a few months later; 'In the opinion of this meeting it is not expedient to encourage the emigration of good labourers by paying the expenses of their passage out of the poor rate. In conformity with the above resolution the application of William Chapman, James Barrow, Thomas Monks, Francis Atkinson shall not be acceded to.'

This was a temporary change of view however and in January 1840 Samuel Packman was allowed £3 for the passage of his child to South Australia and £4 for an

---

[86] Information from his descendant Ted Bryant.

outfit for himself and his family-wife and 3 children- and travel expenses.

In the autumn of 1839 a large family group were preparing to leave the village of Hunton for south Australia. John Haywood and his wife had four sons and four daughters and had cost the parish nearly £24 to support that year.[87]

The local press in Kent sometimes wrote editorials in favour of emigration. In September 1839 the Maidstone Gazette wrote:

'Everything possible ought to be done to disseminate authentic information. The advantages of emigration to all persons whose living depend on their exertions, are so obvious that there is no need of exaggeration. It is time that the labourers of this country were told that there are millions of acres of rich land now lying useless on the other side of the globe; that this waste land belongs to them, but that they cannot reach it without assistance, and that some of the most honourable and benevolent men of the day have undertaken to sell this land...and to pay for the passage of the starving labourers of this country to work on this land.'

The article then criticised some farmers in Kent who managed to get their mens' applications to emigrate turned down because they didn't want to lose such good workers.

---

[87] NA MH12 5196

In the same year a group of villagers were preparing to leave Nettlestead a village in the Maidstone Union for Australia.

'We the undersigned parishioners of Nettlestead consent to emigrate to Australia with our families in consideration of the parish paying the passage money and finding us the necessary Clothes and Tools with £2 each family in money when on board ship.'[88]

Francis Hodges signed and the other three, William Huggitt, Edward Dolding, and Thomas Coulter, being unable to write made their marks. The total financial burden to the vestry for the four families, is listed beneath.

Clothing had of Mr Tomkins Yalding	*£56-12-0*
Passage money to the colony	*£24*
Pocket money £2 to each family	*£8*
Conveyance to Deptford in 3 vans	*£7*
Paid in their journey to Deptford	*£0-14-0*
Mr Tapsfield up with them	*£1-13*
Tools as per bill	*£10-2*
Boxes for tools of Mr Adams	*£0-15*
3pr Blankets given them at Deptford	*£1-10-0*
1pr Trousers for William Huggett	*£0-6-6*
Marriage certificate for Coulter	*£0-2-6*
Marriage certificate for Huggett	*£0-2-6*
Marriage certificate for Hodges	*£0-2-6*
	£111-0-0

---

[88] CKS P262 / 8 / 1

The above Blankets were granted from their having an insufficiency of clothing to be taken on board the vessel at Deptford.'

In the spring of 1842 it seemed that every parish in the Hollingbourne Union had a group of villagers who were preparing to emigrate. They came from Chart Sutton, Lenham, Sutton Valence, Langley, Boughton Malherbe, Detling, Headcorn and Bromfield.[89]

That same year two groups of emigrants left Pluckley, one for New Zealand, the other for Australia. Surprisingly, some were related and yet went to different countries. William Wilmshurst and his wife Sarah, the brother and sister-in law of Eliza Mexted who left for New Zealand, went to Australia. An affectionate and poignant letter from Sarah Wilmshurst to her in laws survives in private hands.[90] Written in 1843, soon after her arrival in Australia it is filled with a longing to see loved ones left behind but also with certainty that they had done the right thing in uprooting themselves, for their circumstances were already much improved.

(I have left the spelling as in the original but added capital letters for clarity.)

'From Adelaide Australia sent 12 September 1842

To William Wilmshurst, Pluckley near Ashford, Old England

Received in Ashford April 1843

---

[89] NA MH12 5136
[90] Reproduced with the kind permission of Phyllis Denne

Dear father and mother

I nowe take my pen to answer your kind letter oping to find you all in good elth as it lives us at present, dear mother whe ar still getting a good living and quite confutabul. Little William John is groing a nise boy and is father said he should like you all to sea him if it should please god. I should be so glad for I shold not be a bit frad for what you wold git a better living here than you do in ingland for here is moore washing put out than there is where you ar, and father might git plenty of farming work here now. Dear mother whe have heard from George and John and they want us to go to them but whe can not leave our home houses and land for whe have got some corn in and ar likey to have a good crop and William is still at the same place weare he gits one pound ten shillings per weak and pivions ar very resonabel here nowe. Dear mother William often sais he wishes he could give you wat we never should never now and it would do you so much good. I wish she where near together for your sake.

Dear mother please give my and William's love to my dear father (Skinner) and brothers an my dear sister and tell my father to let her cum with you if you should com. Tell my brothers I should like to sea them here if they could cum and my father with them. Dear mother I often wish I cold should sea each other in this world I hope and pray we may all be together happy in the world to com where there is no trubel nor ancyty. Dear mother I hope we may all pray and purhaps hear salutes for that happy place where tomorrow never comes.

Dear mother I hope you will rite and send us all the nuse you can and how you ar giting on in this world and how my dear father is gitting on for I think he as so much business that he as forgot that he as a son and dauter in south austrila. Dear father so send me word how my dear brothers ar giting on and my dear litle sister is and wat she is doing and weather she ever sais heny thing about me. Dear mother tell Mary and Carline that they might git places here to nurse and tell Sarah I should like her to play with little William John for he has no body to play with him and tell Amos that here is plenty of better birds here than he used to eat when I was there. O how I wish I cold see you all once moor on this earth Dear mother it is very hot here and many men drink, but thank God I have got a sober partner for he all ways brings me all is mony every sattiday when he gits it and never grumbles to me wat is become of it and that is a comfort to me now I han a way from all my frends that may be a comfort to you all for we live quite happy. So I must conclude my letter and hope it will find you the same way and a good living but I dout it by wat I hire of ingland at present. But I hope it will git better but they tell me there is no hopes of it at present.

So I must now bid you farwell and don't grieve at our leavung you for whe never should got wat we have if whe had stop with you. So she remane your afcant son and dauter William and Sarah Wilmshurst so god by and god bless you and keep you.'

During these years thousands were making their way to Australia without assistance, paying £10 for their passage. In 1841 there was a financial crisis in the colony and the Bounty System was stopped. Altogether more than 26,000 assisted emigrants came out in 1841 and 1842. Some found no work and were no better off than they had been in England, for New South Wales had entered a slump due to drought followed by the raising of land prices by the government.

In Britain the 10th annual report of the Poor Law Commissioners looked back on 1843, during which the total number of emigrants dropped considerably, yet those who left under Poor Law Commissioners sanction for Canada and Australia equalled previous years. The *'re-establishment of the Bounty on Emigration to Sydney and Port Philip in last autumn has been the means of facilitating the emigration of poor persons under our orders... and many parishes have availed themselves of this opportunity of relieving themselves of some of their surplus population.'*

The Commissioners changed one regulation, they no longer required emigrants to Australia to receive landing money from their parishes in order to allow time to find work. The demand for labour was intense and immediate work could be found for all. Assisted emigration to the colony ceased in 1844 and did not recommence until 1847. From 1848 the regulations for assisted emigrants were relaxed and there was help for those who could pay part of their passage. Between 1848 and 1852 New South Wales received 34,110 assisted emigrants from Britain. They were mainly urban and reluctant to leave Sydney, so Kentish farm workers had an advantage in finding jobs further afield. Between 1845 and 1850, 841 people left Kent for Australia on one kind of scheme or another.

In 1846 Throwley vestry had paid the fares and expenses of Martha Raines and three children, Fanny, William and Kitty to Australia where her husband Thomas had been transported four years previously for stealing a sack of meat.[91] She went to join him in Tasmania. The parish borrowed £60 including a generous £8 landing money. Martha and the children were escorted to London and the ship by the Faversham workhouse master and sailed

---

[91] Stevens J, Faversham's reluctant exiles (1996)

in the barque *Psyche*. This situation where a family were assisted to join a man who had been transported did not find favour with the Poor Law Commissioners. In 1840 Emma Newick of Staplehurst had applied for assistance to join her husband in Canada. The clerk of the Maidstone Union wrote to the commissioners:

'her husband was some years previously transported to the colony in question and has since been restored to liberty and his wife and children are about to rejoin him in Canada.'[92]

Of course the commissioners replied that there must have been some error since he could not have been transported to Canada. So in a further letter the guardians explained that Newick had been transported to New South Wales, was pardoned eventually, had made his way to Canada and that since he was no longer a convict they would like to assist the family. The commissioners did not approve.

One can see in the actions of the Poor Law Commissioners that they firmly held on to the concept of the deserving and the undeserving poor. But there was also an over-riding principle to reduce the burden of the poor on the parish rates. As time went on in the 19th century, the ships grew bigger, their health regime improved, journey times became shorter, and the demand for assisted emigration continued. In 1874 the local paper for the Sittingbourne area reported the sailing of the *Derbyshire* with free and assisted passengers to Australia

---

[92] NA MH12 5196

'Queensland emigration.

The ship Derbyshire, 1165 tons sailed from Gravesend 3rd April for Brisbane. Captain Causebrook, surgeon superintendent Dr Watson, matron Miss Davidson. The 133rd vessel that has sailed under the Land Order System. 425 passengers, assisted, remittance and free. 232 members of families, 126 single men, 70 single women.' [93]

The demand for places remained strong especially among Kent's rural communities where jobs in the mills and factories of the industrial towns of northern England did not hold the same attraction as the wide fields beckoning in distant Australia.

---

[93] East Kent Gazette 16.4.1874

New Zealand Pioneers

From the beginning of the 19th century missionaries had been working amongst the Maori people of New Zealand, and encouraged by their reports of the country a new colonising organisation, the New Zealand Company, was formed in London. In 1826 the company sent out the first 70 emigrants in the *Rosanna*. They took livestock, tools and gunpowder to trade for land with the Maoris. The company did not last in this form and in 1837 the New Zealand Association was formed and then reformed in 1839 again as the New Zealand Company.

The company decided to encourage emigration to New Zealand under a similar system to that used in Australia. The New Zealand Company sent Colonel William Wakefield, (brother of Edward), to buy land to sell on to speculators and also to prepare for the arrival of settlers. The money raised by the sale of land would pay for the passage of the emigrants. In 1839 the company appointed agents in large British towns to select people for free passage which was offered in order to attract poor labourers, however there were strict regulations for selection and paupers were not to be eligible. Advertisements tried to attract both gentlemen with cash to invest in land, and 'married mechanics and labourers of good skill and good character.'[94]

---

[94] The Maidstone Gazette, July 16 1839

The regulations of the company, published in May 1840, explained that it would spend 75% of the money received from sales of land to pay for the passage of poorer emigrants who would work for those who bought the land.

'The Company offers a free passage to its settlements, (including provisions and medical attendance during the voyage), to persons of the following description:-viz, agricultural labourers, shepherds, miners, bakers, blacksmiths, braziers and tin men, smiths, shipwrights, boat builders, wheelwrights, sawyers, cabinetmakers, coopers, curriers, farriers, millwrights, harness-makers, boot and shoe makers, tailors, tanners, brick makers, lime burners, and all persons engaged in the erection of buildings.'

The chosen emigrants would have to produce character references and marriage certificates and would be between fifteen and forty. The wives and children under seven would also receive free passage. Single women under thirty were to go free as long as they travelled with relatives or as a servant. Single men could go only if they took an adult sister. All would have to be vaccinated against small pox or to have had it. Every adult was permitted to take half a ton weight of baggage. They had to provide their own outfit of clothes, tools of their trade, and bedding. The clothing list was formidable.

Men	Women
2 jackets	2 gowns or 18 yds printed cotton
2 pr trousers	2 petticoats or 6 yds coloured calico
2 pr duck trousers	2 flannel petticoats or 6yds flannel
2 round frocks	12 shifts or 30yds long cloth
12 cotton shirts	6 caps or 3yds muslin
6 pr worsted stockings	6 neckerchiefs
2 Scottish caps	6 aprons or 6 yds check
6 handkerchiefs	6 handkerchiefs
6 coarse towels	6 towels
1 pr boots with hobnails	1 pr stays
1 pr shoes	6 pr black Worsted stockings
4lbs soap	2 pr shoes
1 pr blankets	1 bonnet
2 pr sheets	Needles, pins, buttons, thread, tape
1 coverlet	4lbs marine soap & 2lbs starch

For each couple a mattress and a bolster, and knife, fork spoon and drinking mug.[95]

Farm labourers and their wives would certainly not have possessed as much and relied upon help from their parishes to equip them.

---

[95] CKS P390 / 18 / 10

Many of the methods used to attract emigrants to Australia were now employed for New Zealand. A surviving poster shows that the company agents visited Kentish villages in 1839 to enlist emigrants. [96]

To receive free passage to New Zealand to sail on the Bolton about 1st November- County Labourers only.

Tuesday October 22nd

Harrietsham 9am, Headcorn 11 am, Staplehurst 1, Goudhurst 4

Wednesday 23rd October

Horsmonden 9am, Brenchley 11, Yalding1, Wateringbury 3 and Town Malling 5

Every emigrant who was accepted by the company had to fill in a form or have it filled in for them, giving a good deal of information including the name of their last employer, a clergyman who knew them and a doctor who knew their state of health. All of which was designed to try to ensure that the company got the type

---

96 NA CO 208 291

of respectable, healthy, hard working settlers they wanted. [97]

Meanwhile Colonel Wakefield was buying thousands of acres of land cheaply from the Maoris but without their full understanding of the transaction. Nevertheless the company decided to send the first 1100 emigrants and they arrived at Port Nicholson in 1840. Port Nicholson, (now known as Wellington Harbour), is a large natural harbour on the southern tip of North Island. Wellington is on the western side of the harbour.

It is thought that between 1839 and 1843 over 8,000 people emigrated to New Zealand under the auspices of the New Zealand Company. Of that total about a thousand had purchased land whilst the rest had free passage with the company as labourers.[98]

The first ships carrying these pioneers were the *Oriental, Aurora, Adelaide,* (these three took many Londoners as well as some Kentish people), the *Duke of Roxburgh* which left Plymouth with emigrants from the west country, the *Bengal Merchant* which carried Scottish emigrants, and the *Bolton* whose passengers included Kentish people. They all sailed to Port Nicholson and landed there before it had been confirmed that enough land purchases had

---

[97] From the Weald to Wellington a history of six pauper families who emigrated from Staplehurst in Kent to Port Nicholson in Wellington arriving in April 1840, D.J. Francis King unpublished thesis for diploma in local history University of Kent 1991

[98] ibid

been made. These first 1100 emigrants including 400 children arrived in January 1840, a week before British sovereignty was established over the colony. The New Zealand Company was rushing settlement in order to buy as much land as possible before government regulations intervened to stop them.

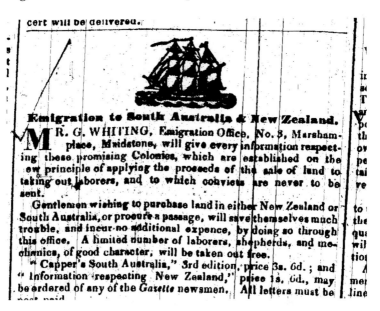

One of George Whiting's advertisements in the Maidstone Gazette for Sep 17 1839

George Duppa of Hollingbourne House, Hollingbourne, an able and confident young man, was one of the New Zealand Company agents. He was the youngest son of the family and so had little money of his own. Being an agent meant that he was paid 40 shillings commission for every married couple who embarked and ten shillings for every single adult who went with their parents. The money was not paid to him until six months after the emigrants arrived in New Zealand. During that time their conduct had to be good or he would forfeit his money, nor would he be paid if the emigrants lacked proper clothes and tools. The other two Kent agents were George Whiting and E.J. Mears. They had to pay for any advertisements put into newspapers themselves.

In September 1840 Whiting wrote to the company, from Maidstone, explaining the difficulties he was having in recruitment because parents had to pay their children's passage money.

'Sir

I have some reason to believe that if you have sufficient confidence in me to give me the power of selecting eligible applicants without payment of the money usually charged for their children I can at this time obtain a considerable number of highly eligible persons. By a letter which Brunger recently wrote to his brother James at Smarden I learned that no emigrant in the depot at the time he was there had paid the money for his children. This information has reached the parochial officers who have at all times evinced great repugnance to pay this money in defiance of the Poor Law Commissioners but who would nevertheless manage to smuggle the expenses of outfit and conveyance for many highly desirable persons...are you and your fellow directors disposed to leave the matter of excusing payment for the children of unexceptionable emigrants to my discretion?...if so I would make extra exertions. I'm so sure some of the best men in the county are anxious to go anywhere to escape from the impending evils of a winter of high prices and unemployment.'[99]

The company soon found that they did have to allow families free passage for their children.

Job Copping of Sutton Valence was one of the men who had been accepted for New Zealand by George Duppa in June 1839 and given £4 by the parish for his and his young wife's outfit. This was after Duppa had sent a letter in support of Copping to the guardians of the Hollingbourne Union.

Hollingbourne House

August 18th 1839

To Mr Reader

Dear Sir,

Job Copping has brought me a few lines from you wishing to know the Name of the ship in which he is to sail. Four ships have been chartered by the New Zealand Land Company and at present it is stated that we shall sail in a Body on the 1st of September from Portsmouth. The Names of three of the ships I can recollect but the fourth I cannot at the moment. The three are the Oriental in which I sail myself, (560 tons), the Aurora (580), The Adelaide (640). I cannot state in which of the 4 ships J Copping and the person who accompanies him will be put, as it rests entirely with the company and cannot be decided until he's married and my nomination given in for him

---

[99] NA CO 208 / 8 / 350

– he tells me his parish objects to assist him even with this trifling sum of £4 for his outfit, but I imagine he must be mistaken – it will be necessary for him to have a sufficient quantity of shirts to last him a voyage of nearly five months, for it must be remembered that he will not be able to have any of his things washed on Board.

He will likewise require some bedding and a few pairs of sheets but his parish must assist him, as I have not it in my power to do so, on account of having done so already to so great an extent.

I am sir yours & etc

Geo Duppa

The Parish had better purchase shirts for J Copping and forward them to this place and I will deliver them to him on board ship.' [100]

Obviously George Duppa had helped some of the emigrants with loans for outfits. He needed to press for a large amount of clothing, as the New Zealand Company had learned from earlier emigration schemes how important it was for the emigrants to arrive with sufficient clothes. How far this was a wish list and how firmly it was enforced is not clear, but obviously as their agent Duppa had to do his utmost to ensure the emigrants he accepted had what was required.

Research shows that Job Copping did indeed marry in September and he and his wife Harriet did sail to New

---

[100] *Hollingbourne Quarterly,* no.27, p.8

Zealand on the Aurora. The witnesses to the wedding in Maidstone, James Farrance and Sophia Streeter were married on the same day with Job and Harriet standing as their witnesses. James and Sophia also sailed to New Zealand on the Aurora. James sadly died in a boating accident soon after arriving at Port Nicholson. In his new country Job Copping became a whaler and seems to have died young in 1850 in an accident at sea.[101]

John Gower a Hollingbourne farm labourer, and his cousin George Pilcher, were also selected by George Duppa, their references being signed by his brother Brian Edward Duppa who was very enthusiastic about New Zealand although he never went there. It was he who strongly recommended that the Nelson area should be the company's second settlement. Pilcher and Gower were amongst the passengers on the *Bolton* and it was whilst on board that John Gower met Mary Ann, a Yorkshire girl. They married upon landing and went on to have their own farm that stayed in the family for many generations.[102]

George Duppa himself sailed on the *Oriental* from Gravesend in September 1839, when he was just 22, with some of the group of Kentish labourers and artisans and their families that he had recruited.[103] A few months earlier he had bought eight properties in Wellington from the New Zealand Company. Each one consisted of one town acre and 100 country acres. When George arrived at

---

[101] Thanks to   Job's descendant Don Herbert of Australia for this information
[102] CKS Duppa papers box 12, uncatalogued
[103] Evans,E. *Hollingbourne and the Duppa family*, 1995

Port Nicholson he found that the land had not yet been purchased from the Maoris. In spite of this he began to fell trees with his group of emigrants about a mile from the sea. A letter George wrote to his sister Fanny in March 1840 explains the difficulties of these first weeks. The valley where they were to settle was a dense forest

'It is now two months since we got on shore and I am not yet out of my tent...the climate appears to be such as an English farmer would pray for, and the soil is such as you would like to have in your flower garden...I intend taking a trip over the hills on a surveying expedition before long to see whether I cannot find some quiet valley, which I can occupy with some few others; and which will not require so large an outlay of capital at starting for I shall not be able to manage the land here until the timber will pay for the clearing.'[104]

Weeks later after being washed out by flood and earthquake, George moved with his group to Oriental Bay Wellington. At Oriental Bay he put up the prefabricated house he had had shipped from England.

Whilst George Duppa had been busy recruiting his emigrants in the Hollingbourne district, the vicar of nearby Staplehurst, the Rev. Thomas Hornbuckle, had been organising the emigration of a group of his parishioners to New Zealand.[105] He cared a good deal for the poor and tried to think of ways to improve their lot. This was not the first time that the vicar had helped

---

104 CKS, Duppa papers, box 12
105 King, D. Arch Cant vol C1X From Staplehurst to Wellington

parishioners to life in a new country. Letters show he had begun in 1829 when he helped a family go to Canada.[106]

When the Poor Law Commissioners received the application for help in sending the Staplehurst emigrants in that autumn of 1839, they wrote to the Colonial Office asking for advice.[107] The commissioners had refused all other applications to New Zealand so far, not feeling that the colony was sufficiently developed to be suitable for groups that would include women and children:

'An application for raising a considerable sum for the emigration of about 40 persons from a parish in Kent has lately come up and the Assistant Commissioner recommends it shall be granted. The Commissioners hesitate and would be glad to receive Mr Stephens advice on the subject.'

W, G Lumley of the Colonial Office replied that

'There is no British colony in New Zealand nor is it yet clear that such a Colony will be established. The government has repeatedly refused to recognise any of the Companies or Associations which have been formed for sending settlers to those islands, Capt Hobson has been accredited to the native Chiefs as H.M.S Consul and has been authorised to negotiate for the surrender to H.M. of the sovereignty of such parts of New Zealand as he may think best adapted as a British Colony, until the result of this negotiation is known, the government must consider New Zealand as a foreign country of which Great Britain has acknowledged the independence and National flag.'

---

[106] CKS P347 / 18/ 11
[107] NA MH 12 5196

So the Commissioners were unable to sanction a loan from the Maidstone Union to Staplehurst parish. They recommended the emigrants be sent to an established colony instead. This was not the only such request the Commissioners received; in June 1840 the parish of Hunton wrote to ask if New Zealand could be considered as a British colony and so as a destination for their poor. The Commissioners replied: 'It has not yet been officially announced to this Board that New Zealand is a British Colony but that they are in expectation of receiving such an announcement..'[108]

However under the influence of the Rev. Hornbuckle, the Staplehurst parish vestry ignored the refusal from the commissioners and went ahead anyway.[109] Parish records show the expenses of 47 emigrants to New Zealand, with clothing at a generous £2 a head, plus subsistence to London paid to George Whiting agent to the `New Zealand Company. The cost to the parish was £118. The New Zealand Company accepted promissory notes from the emigrants to pay their children's passage later.[110] The five families all had children and had all been in difficulties and gone into the workhouse the previous winter.[111]

It has been suggested that Rev. Hornbuckle was encouraged in his New Zealand scheme by the keenness

---

[108] ibid
[109] CKS P347 / 12 / 27
[110] King, D Arch Cant vol C1X from Staplehurst to Wellington
[111] CKS P347 / 12 / 20

of the Duppa family of Hollingbourne whom he knew through several committees. This seems very likely. [112]

The Avery, Nash, Barnes, Farmer and Hunt families from Staplehurst sailed on the *Bolton* from London with about 30 other assisted emigrants from the area in November 1839. The voyage lasted five months during which time one of the Farmer family children died. There were six deaths on the voyage and one birth. The whole group did well in New Zealand, the Avery and Barnes families doing particularly well. Amongst the other Kentish people on the *Bolton* were Thomas Woodman, his wife and family from East Farleigh.

When the *Bolton* docked at Port Nicholson the Kentish labourers settled around the dwelling of George Duppa near the beach; soon moving after suffering first a fire and then a flood, to the site of the present Wellington.

William and Ann Judd and their children from the tiny village of Bicknor near Hollingbourne, had been recruited by George Duppa. They did not go out on the same ship as Duppa but followed months later on the *Martha Ridgway,* sailing from Gravesend.[113] William Judd had an older son, William junior 16, who had sailed out earlier on the *Bolton.*

---

[112] Arch Cant ibid
[113] Information from their descendent D Saywell of Taupo, New Zealand

George Saywell

The Saywells of Bredgar, adjoining Bicknor, accompanied the Judds. George Saywell was a carpenter but had begun his working life by serving as a soldier for two years in the 58th Foot. He and his wife Susan, embarked for their new life with their five young children. George was then 36, and Susan was seven months pregnant. She gave birth to a daughter on the voyage, but the baby, named Martha after the ship, died two months after arrival in New Zealand. Susan had the help of 17 year old Mary Ashby sailing under the Saywell's protection.

The *Ridgway* had a troubled passage with an outbreak of smallpox amongst the 225 emigrants. She set sail from Gravesend in July 1839 and arrived at Port Nicholson in November. The ship and its passengers were taken into quarantine on arrival for three weeks. The new settlement where they were to live was originally called Britannia but the *Martha Ridgway* brought the news that it was to be renamed *Wellington* after the Duke of Wellington.

On arriving at Port Nicholson the Saywells found that the promised accommodation did not exist and so they spent their first nights under a flax bush wishing they had never left home. However the family prospered in New Zealand and soon were in a position to purchase 25 acres of land.

Naturally after George Duppa and his chosen group departed, the Hollingbourne vestry were asked by a number of other poor parishioners for help to go to New Zealand too. So during 1840 a meeting was held in the village to consider raising a poor rate to help villagers to settle in New Zealand the following year, and it was agreed to raise £125.[114] A list was written of those people of the parish who wanted to go. It read:- Richard Mudgway a labourer aged 52 and his wife Ann who was in her forties, their children Charles who was 20, Olive 16 and the younger children, Elizabeth, Stephen, William and Rachel. Then there were their married son George, a labourer, and his wife Elizabeth, another young couple William and Matilda Swaffer and young Daniel Ferles and Elizabeth Alexander who were single. All these were assisted with clothing and with the cost of getting to Deptford to embark as well as the crossing itself. They sailed in the *Catherine Stewart Forbes* on June 10th 1841.

In June 1840 the Maidstone Union guardians again enquired about supporting emigrants to New Zealand and were put off by the Colonial Office. Continued disagreements between the New Zealand Company and the government delayed matters. Nonetheless all over Kent in 1840 groups were preparing to leave for New Zealand. The vicar of Charing wrote in September to the New Zealand Company:

'Charing Maidstone 28 Sep 1840

Sir

In the hurry of my clerical duties yesterday I forgot one essential point viz the £12 for my parishioners' passages. I will...lodge £12 at Ashford bank to be paid to you...... in London. Arrangements have been made for the people to be taken to London in a covered wagon on Monday next 5th October under a proper person appointed by the parish who

---

[114] CKS P187 / 8 / 2

will see them fitted out....The parties will be at the depot on 6ᵗʰ October.

Rev. Ross'[115]

Elderly parents were left behind when their children emigrated under these schemes and of course some found themselves bereft and did not understand that they were too old to be assisted by the New Zealand Company. Such was the case with Frances Seymour of Chatham who wrote this touching letter to Company's London office in September 1840.

'Chatham September 17 1840

Sir

I have taken the opportunity of wrighting to you to let you no that I have maid up my min to follow my Children if possible for I have neither house nor home care. So sir I mean to go and I hop you will order it as soon as you can. Sir I have another relation a strong harty young Woman that wishes to go with me wich will be grat Comfort to me. Sir I hop you will send me an answer by Sunday if you please on account of her leaving her servis and to let me no how to proceed for the best as I am alone Woman now.

Sir I remain yours

Frances Seymour

Direct to Hards Town Cage Lain Chatham'[116]

---

[115] NA CO 208 / 8

It seems one of her sons did not succeed in reaching New Zealand at this time; something went badly wrong, leading to the family being taken off the *London* as this letter from the clerk of the Medway Union to the New Zealand Company shows:

'Medway Union Chatham October 8th 1840

Sir,

I am directed by the Guardians of this union to acknowledge receipt of your bill of expenses incurred in the case of James Seymour and wife who were disembarked from the London. The Guardians are not responsible. Mr Mears the emigration agent sought this family out and induced them to leave Chatham,'

However on the same day that this letter was written old Frances Seymour wrote again to the New Zealand Company a letter of desperation. She cannot have known that one of her sons was returning to Chatham: this time her letter was written for her by someone with a better knowledge of written English:

'Chatham October 8th 1840

Sir

I am utterly at a loss what to do. The parish officers entirely refuse to do anything for me, they will not have the least concern about it I must trust entirely to your goodness and

---

[116] ibid

rely on you for advice. I certainly am a destitute Woman and what of the loss I have lately entertained and being absent from my dear Children the only remaining comfort of my life. Sir I hope I do not to far trespass on your time but I hope nay entreat you to send me word how to proceed has I am confident that the Parish will not render me the least assistance.

Your humble servant

Frances Seymour.'

During 1840 the company received hundreds of letters from would-be emigrants of one kind or another. Occasionally emigrants who had signed up to go were prevented at the last moment. This happened to Thomas Fairbrass of Chartham in September 1840, after a distressing dispute with his wife he sat down to write a painstaking letter to the New Zealand Company :

'Whitewall Chartham near Canterbury

September 7th 1840

Sir,

I am very sorry that I cold not go this month the Reason was because my Wife would not go but my Wife as given Consent to go now we will go in October there is some of my Family gone.

I mean to go in October. Please to write by return of post weather I can go in October and what day the ship go. I will prepare to go.

I am your humble servant

Thomas Fairbrass'

A few days later Thomas Dodds and his family were getting ready to leave their Canterbury home for New Zealand:

'Canterbury September 20th 1840

Sir, I received your letter dated September 17th and please God we are spared life and health we will be at Debtford at the time appointed.

I am sir your obedient servant

Thomas Dodds'.

That year further groups left Thurnham, Lenham and Boxley for New Zealand. One of those from Boxley was Charles Barrow a young poacher who had seldom been in work. The Poor Law Commissioners pointed out that they *'feared it is not the desire to benefit him or the colony...so much as to rid the parish of a troublesome person.'* However Barrow was by then on his way to New Zealand.

In their 7th annual report in 1841 the Poor Law Commissioners wrote of the opening up of New Zealand:

'we did not sanction emigration until her Majesty had assumed the sovereignty of those islands and had established a regular government...we have now for some time sanctioned emigration to that colony, The emigrants have been conveyed thither at the expense of two public companies –the New Zealand Company and the New Plymouth Company and a

considerable portion of the emigrants have come from Kent, Sussex, Devon and Cornwall.'

A British newspaper article of 1841 entitled 'New Zealand described with advice for the labouring classes;' told of the very real prospects available in the colony:

'work here (England) as hard as you will and the chances are you will come to the poor house at last, work there, work and spare not, and you will soon be landlords yourselves.'[117]

It was in 1842, that Captain Arthur Wakefield wrote to the Colonial Office from New Zealand with his concerns:

'We are deluged with emigrants of the labouring class, it is not only absorbing the immigration fund, which will be much required in a few years, but is creating a discontented and pauperish spirit amongst the working class and places me in no very enviable situation having to listen to all the stories that have been told them by the agents.''[118]

The problem was that there were not yet enough employers to employ all the labourers arriving.

A group of farm labourers from Pluckley embarked at Gravesend on the *Lord William Bentinck* for New Zealand on 7th January 1841. Amongst them was George Mexted born in Pluckley in 1806 one of eight children. When he grew up he worked on the local farms and in 1838 married a young widow Eliza Spicer, (nee Wilmshurst), in the parish church. George struggled to earn enough to

---

[117] NA CO 208 / 291
[118] NA CO 208 / 127

support his family and so they decided to try a new life in New Zealand. The parish assisted them to emigrate with their five young children. The two oldest children were from Eliza's first marriage, Thomas who was eight and Elizabeth who was eleven. Baby Eliza Ann was only a few months old, Stephen was three and little George was five.

Amongst the Pluckley group of emigrants were also Eliza's brother and sister John and Harriet Wilmshurst. It was a long slow voyage and it was over four months later when the ship docked at Port Nicholson.

Although he had been a farm worker, George and his family did not work straight away on the land. They lived for the first three years in Wellington whilst saving up to buy their own few acres.[119] In 1844 George was able to buy ten acres of land for £30. It was uncleared land on the road to Johnsonville. In four years the family cleared eight acres and sowed crops. By 1848 they were the proud possessors of two cows and five pigs. George did not stick solely to farming but also contracted for road repair work and for this he employed other men. In 1854 the Mexteds were well enough off to move to a larger farm. They sold their ten acres with the house and farm buildings they had erected themselves. A good profit was made and they were able to purchase 100 acres, they continued to do well and moved several more times. Meanwhile seven more children were born to the family. Both George and Eliza lived long lives in their new homeland.

---

[119] Information on the families lives in New Zealand kindly supplied by their descendant Daphne Guthrie.

Richard Burnett another New Zealand pioneer was born in the village of Borden near Sittingbourne in 1805 and grew up to become a farm labourer. But at the age of 36, in 1841, he sailed away to a new life in New Zealand, aboard the *Whitby*. This ship carried a group of labourers, foremen and surveyors on their way to Nelson to open up a new part of the colony to settlers for the New Zealand Company.

Nelson was the second New Zealand Company settlement. Like Wellington it was on the north coast of the South Island and George Duppa had already taken some Kentish labourers there from Wellington. Duppa had been asked by Colonel Wakefield in June 1841 to accompany Captain Daniell in the *Bailey* to report upon the country and harbours on the Banks Peninsula in order to select a good site for Nelson. However the company directed the settlement to what is now Tasman Bay.

Three ships, the *Whitby*, *Will Watch* and *Arrow* sailed from England a few months ahead of the main group of emigrants to prepare the land for the new settlement. Richard Burnett and his fellow labourers were given free passage and £1-8s. a week pay. This was a grand amount of money as Kentish farm workers were currently earning half that. Richard had to state that he was under thirty as that was one of the requirements of the New Zealand Company; he was obviously an enterprising man, willing to take a risk when it suited.[120]

---

[120] Mrs Nolan of Christchurch, New Zealand

To be selected for the voyage Burnett had had to agree to work in New Zealand for two years. His family had suffered during the previous winter when there was little work available.[121] When he said goodbye to his wife and set sail from Gravesend in April 1841, he knew that she and the children would soon be sent out to join him, meanwhile half of his £1-8s would be paid directly to Sarah. Richard's voyage was a slow one lasting six months.

When the time came for her to join her husband, Sarah was given the money for clothing and conveyance to Deptford by the Milton Union guardians and it was then charged to her parish of Borden. She was Richard's second wife, pregnant with her first child when she embarked on the long voyage in the *Lloyd* in September 1841, accompanied by Richard's two young children by his first wife. The boat was full of the wives and children of the expedition men but whooping cough spread rapidly and half of the 139 children died on the journey. Sarah's baby was born on the ship and died there, christened Richard Atlantic. What a sad journey it must have been for her; by the time she landed her stepson George had also died. On arrival the ship was reported as being badly overcrowded. Captain Wakefield refused to sign the clearance certificate and so neither the doctor nor the captain of the ship could be paid. For his part, Richard had played a role that year in opening up further land in the colony. This created the opportunity for more landowners to take on more employees. It would also

---

[121] NA MH12 5280

allow the New Zealand Company to fulfil its obligations to new emigrants.

The New Zealand Company's 1840 regulations stated

'On the Emigrants arrival in the colony they will be received by an officer who will supply their immediate wants, assist them in reaching their destination, be ready to advise them in case of difficulty, and at all times to find them employment in the service of the company, if from any cause they should be unable to obtain it elsewhere. The Emigrants will, however be at perfect liberty to engage themselves to anyone willing to employ them and will make their own bargain for wages.'

However things did not always go smoothly because such large numbers were arriving so rapidly. By October 1841 when there were 2500 settlers, only 600 were yet farming and, clearing the bush. By then it was clear that there was a big question mark over the settlers' title to the land, which meant that it was not advisable to begin to farm. Matters changed in December 1841 when a million acres were agreed with the Maoris.

Richard and Sarah Burnett settled near Nelson where Richard carried on working as an agricultural labourer and eventually they owned their own house. They had many children. Two years after arrival in New Zealand Richard was involved in a violent confrontation with the Maoris. He had been made a special constable and was sent with a group of other settlers to deal with some Maoris who had burnt surveyors' tents some miles from Nelson. More than 20 settlers were killed and Richard received a bullet wound. However, he survived to live for many more years, dying in 1883.

During months of war with the Maoris in the early 1840s many emigrants decided to leave New Zealand, but some could see that a fortune could be made by grazing sheep. Squatters from Australia imported livestock in the early 1840s and emigrants, tired of waiting for land, invested in flocks and moved onto company lands and squatted.[122] The squatters also leased land at low rates from the Maoris and many of the Kentish emigrants rapidly prospered.

Naturally not all of the early settlers in New Zealand made rapid strides. Problems arose because there were many British absentee landlords whose land remained uncleared and who were not there to employ labourers. Land availability, the acumen and commitment of the new landowners and the supply of skilled labour were all variable factors. The New Zealand agrarian economy developed slowly under the stewardship of the New Zealand Company but even they encountered serious problems. The company had promised £1 a week and rations to unemployed settlers but in January 1843 funds were so low that at least 50 destitute families were sent into the bush to support themselves by farming.[123] Some did well by clearing and farming a few acres and by 1848 a number of former labourers were employing men themselves and labour was short once more.

George Duppa was unscrupulous in his own search for a fortune in the colony and did not endear himself to the settlers there.

---

[122] Kitson, J, The British to the Antipodes
[123] ibid

George Duppa 1818 - 1888

He eventually succeeded in his ambition, but found it a lonely struggle. When he went out he had little money and in fact was helped by a loan of £200 from his sister.[124] In 1852 he wrote from Nelson to his sister Fanny in Hollingbourne appealing to her to write more frequently and saying what pleasure he got from letters from home:

---

[124] CKS U1410 box 30, bundle 3

'I am quite alone, I have no one who has interests in common with me.'[125]

This was after thirteen years in the colony. George was often homesick. He had no friends, and thought many times of returning, but he was set upon first making a fortune and this could not be done quickly. Eventually, after 24 years, he possessed at least 180,000 acres of land and 35,000 sheep, and so returned home to Hollingbourne, ambitions achieved, to become a wealthy country squire. [126]

Agreements continued to be made between Kentish boards of guardians and the New Zealand Company until 1857 when the company was dissolved.

An editorial in the Illustrated London News commented in 1848:

'As a people, it may be truly said of us that we are pre-eminent among the nations of the earth. Our spirit rules the world. Our wisdom enters into the composition of the every-day life of half the globe. Our physical as well as intellectual presence is manifest in every climate under the sun. Our sailing ships and steam-vessels cover the seas and rivers. Wherever we are we conquer, we civilise and refine. Our arms, our arts, out literature are illustrious among the nation. We are a rich, a powerful, an intelligent, and a religious people. No place is too remote for our enterprise or our curiosity. We have an insatiable energy, which is of the utmost value to the world. We have spread ourselves over all regions. We have peopled North

---

[125] CKS U1410 box 30 bundle 11
[126] *ibid.*

America, civilised India, taken possession of Australia and scattered the Anglo-Saxon name and fame, language and literature, religion and law, ideas and habits, over the fairest portions of the globe.

Yet with all this, we maintain in unproductive idleness no less a number than one million and a half of paupers, and have no relief to propose but the compulsory charity of the poor law. We have magnificent colonies that only require labour to be customers for our goods, and aids instead of incumbrances to us; yet we have hitherto devised no plan by which the surplus of the home population shall be drafted to the rich pastures and fertile fields of Canada, the Cape, Australia or New Zealand......

Sooner or later society will recognise the truth that it is not only better but much cheaper to send out armies of industrious colonists to the north, south, east and west, than to maintain armies of idle paupers at home; and that it is folly to allow an enormous population to grow up around us, without debating the mighty question how that population is to be made a blessing instead of a curse.'[127]

The article went on to praise the information the government made available to prospective emigrants, but suggested they could do much more by enrolling factory and school inspectors and poor law officials in the task of actively promoting emigration.

The coming of the age of steam which made tickets for passages cheaper, took away some of the need for assisted emigration for more people could then afford to

---

[127] Illustrated London News July 22 1848

buy their own tickets. However, as we shall see, in Kent the founding of the agricultural labourers' union led to a new wave of assisted emigration in the 1870s. The government still looked kindly on emigration in the 1870s, seeing it as a way both to strengthen the bonds of Empire and also to be rid of the surplus population.

To New Zealand with the Kentish Agricultural Labourers Union

'We would rather go off to New Zealand
Than stay here to starve or to die'[128]

Living conditions for the agricultural labourers of Kent improved little in the years between the 1830s and 1870s. Their average wage of twelve shillings a week had remained unchanged for the previous 30 years. Only families with children old enough to work could earn sufficient for their needs, but for the majority sickness, accidents and old age meant the likelihood of entering the workhouse, whilst in good times they could just get by.

The 1860s saw the first stirrings of trade unionism among the farm labourers in the county. In 1866 the Agricultural Labourers Protection Association was formed in Kent to organise the labourers with a view to improving their working conditions. The association managed to raise wages temporarily in the Maidstone area as this was a year of labour shortage, but then the association faded away leaving no permanent benefits behind it.

By the 1870s farm labourers resented their pay of thirteen shillings a week for 60 hours work which was often lowered when time was lost in bad weather to ten or eleven shillings. To earn full wages labourers were expected to work a 63 hour week. Typically the men

---

[128] Kent & Sussex Times 1.2.1879, from Campion J. 'The emigrants farewell'

walked to work and then did a twelve-hour day before walking home. In many cases this was done on an inadequate diet.

It is easy to understand why many agricultural labourers moved to towns or cities at this time to find other jobs; far more than the numbers of agricultural labourers who emigrated.

All over England farm workers began to organise themselves into unions. The Trade Union Act of 1871 had confirmed that trade unions were legal and gave protection to their funds. Trade unions for skilled town workers were forming. So the time was right for a union to prosper when the Kent Agricultural Labourers Union was founded in 1872 by Alfred Simmons.

The advent of compulsory schooling after the Education Act of 1871 began to deprive the labourers of their children's wages; a grievance mentioned at many Kent meetings of 1872. Labourers did not become entitled to vote for another decade but a new feeling was spreading that by their own efforts they could improve their lives. There is no doubt too that Baptist and Methodist chapels had an influence on the growth of the unions. They were places where many workers learned public speaking and for the first time became involved in the running of an organisation.

Joseph Arch, who had himself been a farm worker, became famous as the leader of the Warwickshire Farm Workers Union early in 1872. In Kent the Kent and Sussex Labourers Union began in April that year as a result of news of Arch's achievements reaching the county. In May 1872 Joseph Arch combined the Warwickshire union with several other counties to form the National Agricultural Labourers Union with himself as president but a few unions such as the Kent and Sussex remained separate.

Alfred Simmons came from a London family cast into poverty during his childhood by the sudden death of his father. The way in which his mother was treated as she struggled to bring up her family resolved Alfred to spend his life trying to improve the lot of the poor.

By 1874 the Kent and Sussex Union had a membership of 9000 with 130 branches and launched its own weekly paper named 'The Labourers Herald.'

The Kent union and the National adopted different tactics. Under Simmons' influence the Kent union favoured a policy of emigration of labourers to New Zealand and Australia where they could make new lives in better conditions. By contrast the priority of the National was 16 shillings a week and the shortening of hours to 9 ½ a day, although they also assisted members to emigrate. Joseph Arch himself visited Canada in 1873 and arranged with the Canadian government for assistance for labourers to emigrate. The union subscribed £1 for a man, ten shillings for a woman and five shillings for a child and the Canadian government paid the rest. Thousands of farm workers and their families were assisted to Canada by the union during the 1870s.

Alfred Simmons' idea was that a policy of emigration would improve the bargaining power of those remaining and to follow this by a wage demand in the spring. This was to prove a successful strategy.

In the autumn of 1872 labourers who had been sacked for joining the union were offered free passage by the government of Queensland. There was considerable demand for manual labourers in Queensland at the time. The Kent Messenger and Maidstone telegraph endorsed the offer saying that agricultural labourers have 'for years been afflicted with poverty, contempt, and ill-usage..Little chance is there in England for a labourer to store sufficient for his old age – he can do so in Australia.' The first group to accept this offer set sail in January 1873.

Between 1872 and 1874 over 50,000 agricultural labourers left Britain, many with families. The autumn of 1872 was a particularly wet one in Kent and the farm workers lost weeks of work and so earned very little. On this pittance it was inevitable that they and their families should go hungry. So there were many who were ready to emigrate to leave poverty and hunger behind. Those who had been enterprising enough to join the union would have been amongst the best farm workers, able to prosper in their new country, a loss to their native land.

The following winter 500 labourers left Kent for Adelaide, South Australia. Soon after this large group had embarked, the South Australian offer of free passage was withdrawn, but was fortunately replaced by an invitation from New Zealand to provide a ship and passage for 350 members of the union and their families.

This was enthusiastically taken up and the departure used by Simmons for maximum publicity for the union. The public were invited to send gifts of clothes and money for the emigrants. The Corn Exchange at Maidstone was booked for the occasion and musicians were employed. A large Christmas tree was set up, hung with these useful presents from the public. After travelling by train to Gravesend and then on to London by steamer, the emigrants at last embarked for New Zealand. Many went on the *William Davie* and the rest on the *Wennington*. The *William Davie* arrived in April 1874. carrying the first group of labourers to New Zealand from the Kent Union.

The New Zealand government was keen to encourage British immigrants in the early and mid 1870s to undertake state sponsored land settlement in the North Island bush. The National Union also sent a large group of emigrants at the end of 1873 on the steam ship *Mongol* and on the sailing ship the *Scimitar* the group contained many families from Oxfordshire and Warwickshire. Between 1873 and 1876 emigrants to New Zealand came more from Cornwall and Warwickshire than any other counties, followed by Kent, Devon, and Somerset.[129] The majority came from the rural counties of southern England.

Close links were formed between the New Zealand government and the Kent union and by the end of the winter of 1873 about a 1000 emigrants had been sent out.

---

[129] Arnold R, Farthest promised land

In February 1874 about 125 sailed on the *Atrato* including 16 families from Burham.

Letters in the union paper such as this one from Thomas Craddock who had belonged to the Headcorn branch must have swayed many families who were thinking of taking the enormous step of leaving all they had ever known behind.

Tarlee South Australia
Sep 18, 1874

Dear Mr Simmons,

I write to thank you and my brother members of the Kent Agricultural Labourers Union for the kindness you showed us before we left our native country but thank God I have not repented for leaving it. This is the country to live in as we don't go to work with half a bellyful out here, nor with any old crust of dry bread for we get plenty of meat to eat with our bread and we can get other things beside meat..we also get more money for when I was in England the money was 16/- 6d per week if you worked all week and out of that we had to pay 2/- or 3/- rent and find our own firing. But here it is quite different as I am getting 25/- a week, house rent and firing...We were eleven weeks coming out and we were not long in getting employment... My mother sent me the Kent Messenger and I was pleased to see that you had got on so well with the great work you have begun of helping the downtrodden labourers of Kent...'

Many such letters were printed in the paper and they showed the depths of privation that the men and their families had suffered in Kent and emphasise the plentiful food and shorter hours in New Zealand. In spite of losing members to emigration, membership continued to increase, most members lived in Kent but there were also 30 branches in East Sussex.

'There is no sixteen hour day out here for a man to work... I wish I had come out here twenty years ago... I am getting ten shillings a day...' Thomas Goodsell, formerly of Plaxtol, wrote from New Zealand. These letters encouraged more to make the big step and two further parties of emigrants supported by the union sailed from London in February 1874 in the *J.N. Fleming* and the *Rooparell*. Then in March 200 sailed in the *Waikato* from Plymouth. Simmons went to Plymouth to see them on their way and there he discovered the *Atrato* returned with engine trouble after travelling a considerable distance. The supplies of the Kentish emigrants on board were running short so Simmons gave the families a sovereign each and the single men half a sovereign. The money came from the recruitment commission for the New Zealand government. All then enjoyed a good voyage.

In spring 1875, a dispute began between farmers and men over wages. Half the Isle of Sheppey's unionists were on the union funds for a while. Discharged by farmers, the union was able to find 30 of them work elsewhere. On 10th July a Sheppey farmer assaulted one of the men and his wife too. The union prosecuted. In August the union assisted 19 to emigrate from the island to Canada. After that the lock-out faded, but it had acted locally as a further spur to emigration.

Thomas Stephens who came from Snodland had his letter from New Zealand printed in the union paper in January 1875. Written in June 1874 to his parents and siblings, it was the first letter they received, for it told of safe arrival in the colony:

'This is a splendid country where we are...We have a little cottage to ourselves but rent is very dear. It is from 8 to 10 shillings a week but wages are from 8 to 10 shillings a day, and work eight hours a day all year round... Meat you can get as much as you can carry for about 3 shillings; suet they give you to carry away.: Bullocks heads and sheep's heads they throw away...This is the place for anyone to be independent if they are careful, for there is plenty here that have only been out about a 12 month, that have got a piece of land, a house of their own, and a nice large garden.'

John Piper was one of the Kentish farm workers assisted to emigrate by the union in 1875. He belonged to the Perry Wood and Oversland branch and wrote a letter to thank them for their help. It was published in the Kent and Sussex Times of October 29th 1878:

'Dear Friends

I have sent you a small sample of our hops we picked last March. The greenest looking were dried in the sun and the others in the kiln. I have every reason to believe that New Zealand will far surpass any other country in the universe in hop growing or anything in an agricultural point of view. Land in New Zealand is being rapidly bought up for farming purposes. There are some of the most splendid samples of wheat, barley, oats and potatoes grown in New Zealand that I ever saw....

Wairoa New Zealand 6.8.1878'

He thanked them for the money they had collected for him. He and his wife Charlotte and six children had embarked on the *Hudson* in 1875 and landed at Napier. He later moved to Wairoa where he had good work setting up a hop and fruit plantation for a settler.

Thomas Harlen a farm worker was assisted to emigrate by the union in 1874. He and his wife Emma sailed in the *La Hague* with their six children. Another child was born as they came into Wellington harbour. Thomas came from Gads Hill.[130]

By October 1874 the union had helped 3000 people to emigrate. During 1875 the Kent union prospered and had several funds with which to help its members such as sickness benefits.

Richard Savage had a letter printed in the union paper in 1878. He had left Burham in 1874 with eight other men, several with families and they were able to help each other in their new lives in Christchurch. Others of course were lonely for familiar faces. Jane Robins had emigrated with her brothers Sam and George from Marden. They were doing well and had no regrets but she longed to be home again.[131] It naturally happened that groups of families from the same village in Kent settled close together in their new country where they could be of help and cheer to one another. Considerable numbers left Kemsing, Wrotham, Rainham, Willesborough, Marden, Brenchley and Lamberhurst at this time.

---

[130] Information from their descendant Lynne Lewis
[131] Arnold R, Cantium winter 1974, A Kentish exodus

Kent's farmers were uneasy with the growth of the union and the new self-esteem it gave the men. By January 1878 the union had 14000 members. Prices were falling and rents rising so the farmers decided to take the union on. They planned a lock-out for 1878 aimed at breaking the union. Alfred Simmons felt that wealthy landowners were behind it, putting pressure on their tenant farmers to lower wages- men such as Lord Darnley and Hart-Dyke in west Kent, the Neames and Lakes in east Kent. So in October 1878 the farmers reduced wages by 1/6 a week. The union called out its men and the number of members locked out for refusing to accept reductions rose to 900 by mid December.

The union supported the men and there was a good deal of public support. Mass meetings were held in Canterbury and Maidstone and members marched to London. When the union began its wages campaign there were no further lockouts. Farmers were approached branch by branch and there was agreement. Simmons' well thought out policies contributed much to the continuing success of the Kent union. Public sympathy grew when several farmers began eviction proceedings against labourers in tied cottages.

Fortunately the timing of the lock-out had coincided with a surge in demand for agricultural workers in New Zealand, and the New Zealand Agent-General in London, Sir Julius Vogel had cabled the New Zealand Prime Minister in November:- *'Kent and Sussex labourers have struck; seems splendid opportunity obtaining immigrants. Could send several hundred by steamer arrive Feb., or later by sailing vessels'.* Both the union and the New Zealand authorities were keen to move fast.

Alfred Simmons had taken the decision to go with the families to New Zealand and his decision probably encouraged some of the labourers to go. He had met with the New Zealand emigration authorities and in December was able to tell the meetings of free passage arranged for 700 farm workers and their families.

Simmons naturally used the union newspaper, The Kent and Sussex Times, to encourage members to emigrate. Nevertheless there was still difficulty in getting the required number of people, and New Zealand officials had to make up the numbers with emigrants from elsewhere in England. They were to leave Maidstone for Plymouth on January 29th. About 400 came from the Kent and Sussex Union. Each was given £1 from union funds and most were given a little extra cash by branch members.

The party were to undertake the voyage in the *Stad Haarlem*, a modern iron steam ship built in Glasgow. This was only the second steam ship to take emigrants to New Zealand and had been selected as the workers were needed to arrive in New Zealand in time for the harvest.

Of the labourers who decided to leave Kent on this occasion a number came from the Brenchley and Lamberhurst area of the Weald where the farmers had taken a very hard attitude against the union. More left east Kent, especially the area around Faversham, which had been at the heart of the lockout. Matters had been particularly difficult in Chilham and Chartham where a number of men had been threatened with eviction.

In deciding to accompany the emigrants to New Zealand, Simmons was following the precedent set by Joseph Arch, who had been to Canada where the National Union had assisted many members to settle. But unlike Simmons, Arch was not keen on emigration. He wrote in his autobiography:- *'I only looked upon emigration as a disagreeable necessity, not as a thing to be recommended. I could not bear to see our best men pouring out of the mother country when I knew we wanted them badly'*. This was written after his visit to Canada.

Those who were to sail in the *Stad Haarlem* met in Maidstone at the Assembly Rooms where there was a farewell meeting with speeches and music and singing. No doubt this was an occasion for the singing of The Emigrants Farewell written by an emigrant from Chartham, later printed in The Kent and Sussex Times. Written in January 1879, there were seven verses and a chorus which ran:-

'Farewell to the labourers union
Farewell to its leaders and all
Farewell to all friends in old England
We must now bid adieu to you all"

The song expressed the hope that

'We shall soon be at home o'er the water
And then have work plenty to do
And get wage in proportion to labour
For all that our hands find to do'

That night the women and children slept at the skating rink and the men went to lodgings. After breakfast the whole party, marched with banners to the station. There must have been many scenes of sad farewell from relatives left behind before the train moved off on its ten hour journey to Plymouth and the emigration depot. About 90 of the party were single men, the rest families. All wanted to better themselves.

For most it was to be a successful voyage with little ill-health, although four babies died. Simmons kept a diary while away from home, for publication in the newspaper. Some of this was then added to his account of his stay in New Zealand to become the book, 'Old England and New Zealand', published in 1879. The diary shows that he set off feeling that it was a dangerous journey, but he was much encouraged by all the good wishes and presents he received from people he had never met before. He felt he was doing his duty:

'I should be a poor leader to those I have taken by the hand, were I to shrink from a journey which presents itself, to my mind as a matter of duty, however dangerous this journey may be.'

In fact he was rather exaggerating the dangers. Voyages were far safer than in earlier years and in addition he travelled as a saloon passenger in much more comfort than his union members. Like many others, he suffered from seasickness. In the Bay of Biscay they encountered a great storm, the hatches were battened down and no one allowed on deck, but by the time they passed the Canary Islands on February the 21st., the weather was good and everyone felt much better. Simmons remarked upon the fact that when the first religious service was held less than 50 emigrants turned out to be Church of England members, the rest were Nonconformists of one kind or another. Games were held on board to pass the time as the voyage continued and entertainments were put on in the evenings.

The ship arrived at Lyttleton on April the 14th 1879 where the emigrants for the South Island disembarked and where Simmons, was met by a crowd of men,

'They were men from Kent, who had formerly left for New Zealand and who had come up from the country with their wives to bid me welcome... and thus after our two months voyage, we at last found a cordial reception from Kentish friends 14,000 miles away from home.'

The rest of the *Stad Haarlem* passengers were landed at Wellington on the 18th. The immigrants were described as being of a 'very desirable class' and very keen to work.[132] Demand for labour had already dropped by the time the Stad Haarlem arrived, but many of the new arrivals were sent on to Patea, where new land was being opened up and, later on, many had a chance to buy land and prospered.

As Simmons travelled the country he talked to hundreds of men from Kent who had already been in the colony for several years. Their wages were good. Single men were earning £1 to 25 shillings per week, having food and accommodation free. There were married men on £60 to £100 per annum, but house rents could be as high as nine shillings per week for a small house. On the other hand

---

[132] Anold R, Cantium ibid

food was very cheap, especially meat, since beef was five pence a pound and mutton three. The families were glad they had come, many now owned a house and land and had sent for elderly parents to live with them.

However Simmons could see that the time for agricultural labourers to leave in large numbers in order to settle in New Zealand was coming to an end. On his return to England he was welcomed back by 35000 people at Rochester, reflecting the union members' great affection for him. [133]

This advertisement appeared in the East Kent Gazette at the start of 1878 showing that Simmons was also an emigration agent for Queensland.

Queensland emigration
Sailings from Great Britain

The next ship the *Ironsides* for Brisbane sails from London on Jan 31st. Female domestic servants and farm labourers free. Apply to the local agent A. Simmons 115 Week Street Maidstone or to the agent general for Queensland 32 Charing Cross Road London S.W

Free emigration to New Zealand was ended by its government in August, 1879. Members of the union continued to emigrate in 1880 on non-union grants and personal initiative, though no longer in large groups.

---

[133] Kent & Sussex Times 19.7.1879

When the *Stad Haarlem* sailed there were still men left behind who were on the lockout supported by the union. But a month after she sailed only just over 200 remained locked out. Many letters were published in the union paper in the months after the arrival of the *Stad Haarlem* from the emigrants all telling of their good prospects, their better pay, the plentiful cheap meat.

Simmons turned his attention to the National Association for Promoting State Directed Colonisation, founded in 1883, of which he was the Secretary. Simmons' union backed the State Directed Colonisation Scheme. In 1886 he published, 'State Directed Colonisation, the Proposal Explained and Defended,' which was one of a series of booklets by various authors.

He laid out the reasons why emigration was a good idea, such as the growing population, unemployment and mechanisation. Free passages to the colonies had largely ceased, but Simmons said he would not be a party to over-stocking the colonial labour market, there would have to be a need for the emigrants' labour. The idea of state-directed colonisation, he explained, was to allow our hard-working surplus population to go to the British colonies and for them to repay the loan of money they received to take them there. But, '*the very head ...of our proposal is, that land must first be provided upon which to plant the people who depart from the mother country.*' Simmons' system was approved as a proposal put forward by a deputation from the National Association to Earl Granville, Secretary of State for the Colonies and the Under-Secretary of State for the Colonies, in 1886.

There was certainly still a demand for assisted passages to the colonies at this time, helped no doubt by articles such as that which appeared in The Home Visitor, a national weekly church magazine, during 1885. Here, reporting on New Zealand emigrants, the writer found:

'Every efficient labourer and every decent girl obtained employment at once and the wages were invariably in excess of those stated by the Government prospectus. Such was the demand on every hand for labour, that builders, farmers, and others were at their wits' end to know how to obtain the requisite help.'

The article extolled the good wages, cheap food and land and lack of poverty.

By the mid 1880s free and assisted passages to Canada, New Zealand, New South Wales, Queensland and south Australia had largely been discontinued, though there was to be another great surge in emigration in the early years of the twentieth century.

Simmons eminent career came to a tragic and shocking end in 1887, when, still only 41, he appeared before a Maidstone court charged with withholding money from the union and fraudulently misapplying money. His public career was finished and though he paid the money within the week his name was erased from the union roll. The evidence certainly points to a discrepancy in the accounts, but it is impossible to believe that after years of devotion to the union and its members Simmons would actually take money from them. Perhaps a genuine mistake occurred, followed by a stubborn proud refusal to admit it. Whatever the truth of the matter, the affair finished Simmons' career and meant personal anguish. What happened to Simmons and his family in later years is not known. It may be that he changed his name and lived in another part of England. Perhaps only his descendants know the rest of his story. He deserves to be remembered in Kent for the contribution he made to the welfare of poor farm labourers and the help he gave them to emigrate to a better life in New Zealand.

Postscript

Rural Kentish parishes helped their poorest inhabitants to emigrate from the 1820s onwards. Assisted emigration before the advent of the Poor Law Act was haphazard, depending on the attitude of local individuals and on funds available. Bad harvests, low pay and periods of unemployment spurred people to consider emigrating, though the perils of the journey and the consequent risks to health and survival had also to be weighed in the balance.

As the 19th century progressed, the risks were lessened. Better and faster ships, shorter journey times, improved survival rates and better provisions, ensured that more people faced the voyage with confidence. They also felt more assured about the outcome in the new territories where better opportunities and employment gave them a grip on their new lives.

Their letters back home spurred more to go and so fresh waves of emigrants followed in the footsteps of the pioneers. In some cases whole local populations from Kent were transplanted into new localities on the other side of the world. Many were able to make great contributions towards the building of their adopted homelands and to ensure better futures for their children and grandchildren. We can look back with admiration from our affluent present at all the hardships they endured and overcame in their struggles to improve their lives.

Appendix One – Assisted emigrants from Kent parishes

Information taken from annual reports of the Poor Law Commissioners

Assisted emigrants from Kent parishes 1835- 1845
(These figures include children)

Assisted emigrants from Kent parishes between July 1835 and July 1836

Barham	23	United States
Benenden	5	New York
Brabourn	8	New York
Cheriton	43	Upper Canada
Chislet	16	New York
Egerton	26	Upper Canada
Elmstone	1	Upper Canada
Folkestone	28	Upper Canada
Gt Mongeham	10	Upper Canada
Headcorn	8	Upper Canada
Lenham	23	Upper Canada
Newington	22	Upper Canada
Otterden	9	Upper Canada
Preston, nr Wingham	7	Mansfield
St Lawrence	5	Upper Canada
Throwley	12	Canada
Ulcombe	30	Canada
Saltwood	8	Baltimore
Saltwood	36	Upper Canada
Total	**320**	

Assisted emigrants from Kent parishes between July 1836 and July 1837

Cheriton	1	Canada
Egerton	20	Canada
Harrietsham	4	New York
Hever	12	Upper Canada
Hunton	12	Hobart Town
Hunton	5	Montreal
Lenham	19	Upper Canada
Molash	9	Upper Canada
Stockbury	39	Upper Canada
Ulcombe	31	Upper Canada
Warehorne	4	Canada
Total	**156**	

Assisted emigrants from Kent parishes between July 1837 and July 1838

Benenden	5	United States
Bethersden	12	Australia
Goudhurst	8	Canada
Hawkhurst	19	Australia
Kingsnorth	8	South Australia
Rolvenden	78	Australia
Sandhurst	92	Australia
Stone	9	Australia
Wittersham	8	Canada
Woodchurch	12	Australia
Total	**251**	

Assisted emigrants from Kent parishes between July 1838 and July 1839

Aldington	4	Australia
Appledore	11	Australia
Benenden	34	Australia
Brookland	16	Australia
East Peckham	6	Australia
Egerton	6	Australia
Great Chart	5	Australia
Headcorn	3	Australia
Langley	3	Australia
Lydd	8	Australia
Lympne	19	Australia
Mereworth	7	Australia
Mersham	8	Australia
Newington	5	Australia
Rolvenden	93	Australia
Sellinge	6	Australia
Smarden	7	Australia
Smeeth	1	Australia
Speldhurst	8	Australia
Tenterden	9	Australia
Warehorne	5	Australia
Woodchurch	43	Australia
Total	**307**	

Assisted emigrants from Kent parishes between July 1839 and July 1840

Parish	Number	Destination
Benenden	49	New South Wales
Biddenden	15	South Australia
Bilsington	10	South Australia
Bonnington	4	New South Wales
Boxley	5	South Australia
Chart	5	Canada
Chevening	7	South Australia
Goudhurst	28	South Australia
Hawkhurst	36	Canada
Hunton	10	South Australia
Kenardington	12	New South Wales
Leeds	7	New South Wales
Hythe	4	New South Wales
Lydd	9	South Australia
Mersham	8	New South Wales
Nettlestead	28	South Australia
Peckham E	22	South Australia
Ruckinge	6	South Australia
Saltwood	7	South Australia
Sevington	2	South Australia
Smarden	7	South Australia
Sutton Valence	10	Upper Canada
Tenterden	3	New South Wales
Trottiscliffe	11	South Australia
Yalding	24	South Australia
Total	**329**	

Assisted emigrants from Kent parishes between July 1840 and July 1841

Boughton Monchelsea	17	Sydney
Chart Sutton	25	Canada
Eastbridge	7	Australia
Frittenden	10	New Zealand
Goudhurst	39	New Zealand & Australia
Hawkhurst	10	Sydney
Hollingbourne	15	New Zealand
Lydd	4	Port Phillip
Marden	51	New Zealand
Pluckley	26	New Zealand
Smarden	16	New Zealand
Ulcombe	18	Canada
West Peckham	5	New Zealand & Sydney
Westwell	17	New Zealand
Wye	3	Sydney
Yalding	35	Sydney
Total	**298**	

Assisted emigrants from Kent parishes between July 1841 and July 1842

Parish	Number	Destination
Aldington	16	Australia & Canada
Appledore	5	Canada
Aylesford	6	Australia
Bearsted	not given	
Benenden	15	Canada & N Zealand
Biddenden	62	Canada
Borden	4	New Zealand
Brenchley	31	Canada
Chart	not given	
Faversham	not given	
Frittenden	not given	
Goudhurst	12	Australia Canada N Zealand
High Halden	10	Canada
Hawkhurst	14	New Zealand
Headcorn	15	Canada
Hurst	not given	
Hythe	15	Australia
Leeds	7	Canada
Lenham	10	New Zealand
Linton		New Zealand
Lydd	not given	
Milton	not given	
Monks Horton	8	Australia
Newchurch	4	Australia
Sandhurst	26	Australia & Canada
Staplehurst	11	Australia
Sutton Valence	not given	
Tenterden	9	Canada
Thurnham	4	Australia
Tong	not given	
Wittersham	42	Australia & Canada
Total	**more than 327**	

Assisted emigrants from Kent parishes between July 1842 and July 1843

Benenden	6	New Zealand
Bethersden	8	Canada
Boughton Malherbe	18	Canada
Boxley	1	New Zealand
Chart	14	Canada
Detling	8	New Zealand
Faversham	7	Canada
Goudhurst	2	Canada
Hawkhurst	9	Canada
Headcorn	37	Canada
Hollingbourne	8	Canada
Hollingbourne	2	New Zealand
Langley	18	Canada
Leeds	8	Canada
Lenham	32	Canada
Lydd	29	Canada
Selling	14	Canada
Sutton V	21	Canada
Tenterden	47	Canada
Tong	2	SouthAustralia
Ulcombe	6	Canada
Total	**297**	

Assisted emigrants from Kent parishes between July 1843 and July 1844

Benenden	28	Canada
Biddenden	11	Canada
Gt Chart	4	Canada
Chislett	4	Canada
Davington	8	Canada
Dunkirk	6	Canada
Faversham	13	Canada
Goudhurst	11	Canada
Hawkhurst	15	Canada
Headcorn	8	Canada
Langley	1	Canada
Lenham	7	Canada
Newchurch	7	Canada
Ospringe	8	Canada
Sandhurst	32	Canada
Stockbury	2	Canada
Tenterden	1	Canada
Throwley	7	Canada
Wittersham	4	Canada
Woodchurch	16	Canada
Total	**193**	

Assisted emigrants from Kent parishes between July 1844 and July 1845

Goudhurst	18	Canada
Hawkhurst	1	Canada
Tenterden	2	Canada
Wittersham	7	South Australia
Total	**28**	

Assisted emigrants from Kent parishes between January and December 1845
(in addition to those above)

Buckland	4	Canada
Maidstone	9	Australia
St Mary	11	Canada
Wootton	12	Canada
Total	**34**	

Appendix Two – Named assisted emigrants with their home parishes

Names have been found either in parish or poor law union records. These lists do not imply that these were the only emigrants from this parish.

Aldington	**1838**	**Australia**
William & Sarah Thomas & children		
Aldington	**1841**	**Australia**
Richard Bartlett, wife & children		
Aldington	**1850**	**Australia**
Widow Straky & 6 children		
Appledore	**1834**	**America**
George Bourne & wife		
Appledore	**1838**	**Australia**
James Holdstock, wife & child		
William Hixton, wife & children		
Ashford	**1838**	**Australia**
Joseph Hart, wife & children		
Aylesford	**1841**	**Australia**
George Stedman, wife & 4 children		
Benenden	**1838**	**Australia**
John Baker, wife & children		
William Beach & wife		
William Bryant, wife & 7 children		
George Butler, wife & children		
Jesse Butler, wife & child		
William & Elizabeth Bowden		
Thomas Chapman, wife & children		
John Clovet, wife & children		
John Crittenden, wife & children		
William Gilbert, wife & children		
William Goodwin, wife & children		

Bethersden	**1838**	**Australia**

Clarke Harman, wife & children

Bicknor	**1840**	**New Zealand**

William Judd, Ann wife, William 16,
John 8, George 6, Stephen 3

Biddenden	**1827**	**America**

William Manerings, wife & 2 children
Joseph Pilbeam, Richard Curtis
John Ellis, wife, 4 children
Edward Ellis & wife
David Becken, wife, 1 child

Biddenden	**1833**	**America**

Samuel Paine wife & children

Biddenden	**1838**	**Australia**

Joseph Whatman, wife & child

Biddenden	**1840**	**Canada**

Edward Brazin, wife, 2 children

Biddenden	**1842**	**America**

Stephen Well, & wife
Mary 18, George14, Anne10
Mrs Mackelden widow of William
William 18, Harriet 13
James10, Jane 8
Seaman Smith, wife & child

Bobbing	**1838**	**Canada**

Thomas Croucher wife & 6 children

Borden	**1842**	**Canada**

Richard Ingram wife & children
John Ingram wife & children

Borden   **1849**   **Australia**
Thomas Rayfield & family
Elizabeth French
Mary Anne Luckhurst
John Baldock wife & 4 children

Boughton   **1841**   **Australia**
Monchelsea
William Waterman wife & 11 children
William Morris wife & 2 children

Boxley   **1841**   **New Zealand**
William Sunnocks, wife & 5 children

Brookland   **1838**   **Australia**
Henry Viner & wife

Burmarsh   **1828**   **America**
John Hogbin, wife & 3 children

Burmarsh   **1834**   **America**
John Whitehead, wife & 5 children
Richard Whitehead, Anslow Sharpe

Charing   **1841**   **Australia**
Joseph Coppins, wife & children

Chart Sutton   **1840**   **Canada**
James Brown 26, Mary 24 & children
George Brown 36, Sarah 13
George 12, William 10
Elizabeth 9, Frances 5, Jemima 3
Edwin Shirley 29, Sophia, 28
Edwin, Elizabeth, John & Samuel
John Brown, 31, Hannah, 27
Ann, John, George, Hannah & Lucy
Mary Burden, 19

Chartham	**1828**	**America**
William Craig, wife 3 children		
Cranbrook	**1838**	**Australia**
William Harris, wife & children		
East Farleigh	**1839**	**New Zealand**
Thomas Woodman, wife & family		
Egerton	**1827**	**America**
John Landen & family		
William Turk & family		
Benjamin Ballard & family		
James Palmer & family		
Egerton	**1849**	**Cape of Good Hope**

Thomas Dawkins 40 labourer
Margaret Dawkins 36
Jane 16, Elizabeth, 9
Richard 7, Mary Ann 2

Frittenden	**1841**	**New Zealand**
Samuel Tolhurst, wife & children		
Frittenden	**1844**	**Canada**
John Arum? wife & 4 children		
George Ransom wife & 2 children		
George Tolhurst		
Goudhurst	**1849**	**South Africa**
William Roberts, wife & 6 children		
Charles Crittenden & family		
Thomas Golding & family		
George Crittenden & family		

Herne   **1852**   **Canada**
William Pibus 35 sawyer
John 8, Elizabeth, Sarah 10, Ann 3
Hollingbourne   **1842**   **New Zealand**
James & Elizabeth Wratham
Hollingbourne   **1842**   **Canada**
William Bennett
William Judd, Harriet & 5 children
Hunton   **1839**   **Australia**
John Haywood wife & 8 children
Hunton   **1840**   **Australia**
William Taylor 44, wife & 6 sons
Hythe   **1838**   **Australia**
Edward Crouch & wife
John Sexby & wife
George Sexby & wife
Leeds   **Canada**   **1842**
Gibbons family, 2 Hollands
1 Munn
Lenham   **1853**   **Australia**
William & Elizabeth Sage & 4 children
Linton   **1843**   **New Zealand**
Robert Burgess 30, Phoebe 32
Jane 12, William 10, Israel 8, Selena 5
Charles Pettit 39, Elizabeth 39
William 15, Charles 14, Thomas 11
Elizabeth 12, Ann 9, George 8,
Emily 7, Samuel 3, Edward 1, Mercy infant
George Quinnel 36, Mary 30, George 12,
Mary 9, Charles 3
Molash   **1839**   **Canada**
James Rogers wife & children
Nettlestead   **1840**   **Australia**
Thomas Coulter 35, Frances 39,

Timothy, Thomas, Lewis?, Robert, Mary, Elizabeth
William Huggett 38, wife 2 sons 3 daughters
Francis Hodges 39, wife, 4 sons 2 daughters
Edward Dolding 26, wife & 2 sons

Ospringe **1835** **Upper Canada**
John Moone, wife & 2 children
Cephas Quested, wife & boy
George Moone, Thomas Dunk
Charles Anderson, William Moone
James Harrison, Thomas Barnett
Mary A Graves, Jesse Prickett
James Prickett, Robert Bones

Ospringe **1835** **New York**
William Foster wife & 6 sons

Ospringe **1843** **Canada**
William Cutting 34, Mary A 28, William 9, John 8,
Thomas 7, George 5, Henry 2, Sarah Wellard 18

Pluckley **1841** **New Zealand**
George Mexted 34, Elizabeth 30 & 5 children
John Wilmshurst & Harriett

Preston-next- **1849** **Australia**
Faversham
Edward French 32, Elizabeth 25, James 5, Emily 7m

Preston-next- **1836** **Canada**
Wingham
George Spain, wife & 5 children

Rolvenden   1838   Australia

James Austen, wife & children
Thomas Austen, wife & children
George Austen & wife
Edward & Maria Blanch
George Blanch, wife & child
Isaac & Sarah Blanch
Thomas Drury, wife & child
Jesse Judge, wife & children
Edward Marshall
William Moon snr, wife & children
William Moon jnr & wife
John Shoebridge, wife & child
George Shoebridge

Saltwood   1836   Canada

John Smeed 42, Mary 43
Richard Smeed 20, Mary 12
Charlotte 14, William 12, John 10, Hannah 6, John? 4,
Robert 2
George Hams 35, Eliza 26, John 7
George 5, Eliza 2, William 1
Richard Webb 60, Sarah 48, Jane 14, George 10, Thomas 7
Robert Ward 29. John Young 22, William Booth 20,
Barling Giles 19, Philip Finn 17

Saltwood   1836   New York

Thomas Johnson 46, Mary 37
William 20, Thomas 17, John 15, Mary Ann 9, Charles 7,
Richard 7m

Sandhurst   1826   America
George Fuller, Jemima & 5 children
James Harris 26, Mary & 2 children
Charles Wenban 29, & wife
David Smith, George Smith jnr 19
John Mainard, Samuel Simmonds
George Wybourn, William Harris
Sandhurst   1827   America
Longley Coleman 28, Harriet 21,
Thomas, Elizabeth
John Lavender, Elizabeth
John 11, Mary 9, Thomas 5, Harriet 2
William Mainard jnr 23
Henry Mainard 17
William Mainard snr 48, Hannah 45
Joseph12, Eliza 11, Richard 9, Hannah 7
Samuel 5, Stephen 2
William Wenban 25, James Wenban 20
Edward Wenban 18
Henry Sivyer 20
William Edmunds 22
Sandhurst   1828   America
John Wybourn, Martha
Martha 25, John 22
William 19, Mary Ann 17
Sarah 10, Gerard 8
Robert 5
Stephen Swatland & Sarah
Stephen 9, James 7
Soloman 5, Spencer 3
Samuel 1

Sandhurst   1838   **Australia**
William & Sarah Avard, 4 children
Charles Clark & wife
Thomas Haines, wife & children
William Hashenden, wife & children
Mary Ann Martin
John Robard snr, Martha wife
James, Henry, & Aaron
John Robard jnr, wife 2 children
Wm Robard wife, 1 child
Stephen Robard wife 1 child
George & Mary Wattus
William Wenban & wife
Sandhurst   1839   **Australia**
James Robards, Sarah, James 17
Sarah 16, John 8, Harriott 13
Edward 3, Emma 11, Mary 8
Martha 4
Sandhurst   1841   **Canada**
William Catt, wife & children
Croft family, Vidler family
Staplehurst   1829   **Canada**
Edward Hickmott, wife & 6 children
Staplehurst   1830   **America**
M Pearce

Staplehurst　　　　1839　　　　　New Zealand
Thomas Avery 37, Elizabeth 40, George 16, Charles 14,
Stephen 2, Harriet 18, Ann 11, Mary 9, Sarah 7, Ellen 5
John Farmer 41, Mary 33, John 16, Jesse 12, James 11,
Mary 4, Ann 1
William Hunt 38, Hannah 34, Edward 13, Stephen 10,
Richard 9, Charles 7, James 4, Mary Ann 15, Sarah 2
John Nash 26, Norman 3, George 1, Ann 25, Miriam 5
William Peckham 44, Mary 44, William 15, James 6,
George 1, Mary 17, Caroline 11, Adelaide 8
Robert Relf 38, Ann 35, James 13, Robert 11, William 4,
Sarah 8, Ann 6, Mary 1
Robert Gilbert 23

Stockbury　　　　1837　　　　　Canada
William Gibbs 23
William Beecham 25, Mary 23
Leonard Lambkin 66, Elizabeth 65
Moses Whitehead 17
James Burr 35, Hannah 35, William 16, Caroline 9, James
8, Eliza 2
Thomas Gransden 27, Amy 27 William 6, Frances 7m
Richard Lambkin 34, Rebecca 36, Leonard 14, John 12,
Mary 10, Martha 8, Nicholas 6, Elizabeth 3, George 1¾
Stephen Lambkin 23, Frances 25, Sarah Ann 4, and
Elizabeth 1
George Mills 33, Ann 30, James 9, Jane 6, Mary Ann 4,
George, Alfred 1
George Standen 22, Sarah 21
William Syflet 35, Jane 33

Stockbury   **1843**   **Canada**
Richard Beecham, John Beecham
Stone-in-Oxney   **1838**   **Australia**
Joseph & Mary Dunster, Joseph, Walter, Humphrey, Mary, Sophia, Charlotte
Richard Denness 29, Sarah 27
Sarah 6, Ruth 1, Adam 4
John Morphett 26, Frances 29, John 4, George 1
Sutton Valence   **1840**   **Canada**
Jesse Bafsage 21
John Baker, 26, Eliza21
George Tapsell, 29, Charlotte 29
Jane 4, Esther 2, James 9m
Tenterden   **1838**   **Australia**
John & Mary Gilbert
Teston   **1838**   **Australia**
Richard Honey, wife & 2 children
Tong   **1842**   **Australia**
James Moore & wife
Tong   **1852**   **Canada**
William Hope wife & children
James Hope wife & children
Throwley   **1846**   **Australia**
Martha Raines,. Fanny 14, Wlliam 10, Kitty 6
Wateringbury   **1832**   **Canada**
John Beadle, wife & family
Thos Barlow, Richard Latter
Phillip Pound, Daniel Sudds
John Murphy

Wateringbury   1838   Australia
John Lamb, wife & 2 children
John Fielder
Henry Clout, wife & children
Westerham   1832   America
Robert Smith, wife & children
Robert Bateman, wife & child
Fuller & wife
William Bynold
West Farleigh   1839   Australia
William & Elizabeth Fry & 4 children
West Peckham   1841   NewZealand
William Forrester & family
Wittersham   1838   Australia
Richard Apps & wife
William Apps & wife
Woodchurch   1838   Australia
Benjamin Hampton, wife & children
James Heckins, wife & child
Yalding   1835   America
Thomas Maynard & family
Yalding   1839   Australia
John Cheeseman 34, Barbara 36, Thomas 15, James 8, Lydia 12, Eliza 6, Mercy 4, Susannah 10m
Yalding   1840   Australia
Henry Savage 37, Rebecca 36, John 19, William 17, Henry 6, Daniel 1, Rebecca 15, Mary 11, Elizabeth 3
Robert Smith 39, Frances 36, George 6, Cordelia 16, Frances 10, Catherine 4

Yalding **1841** **Australia**

Thomas Fuller 37, Elizabeth wife 34, Lydia 13, William 1

Jesse Jones 26, Sarah, wife 28, John 19m

William Pope 28, Mary Ann 28 wife

Caroline 2, William 2m

Mary Ann Cornford 8, Sarah Cornford 7

James Reader 37, Mary, wife 37, Hannah 8, James 2, Amos 1

John Spice 38, Mary 28 wife, John 12, Jonathan 4, Edwin 2, Charlotte 8, Esther 6

William Thorncroft 37, Sarah 24 wife, Reuben 4, Sophia 1

Thomas Tompsett 35, Susanna 29 wife, Ansley 12, Harriet 10, Mary Ann 7, Elizabeth 1

Bibliography

Allinson H   Borden the history of a Kentish parish
                 (2003)
Allinson H   Bredgar the history of a Kentish parish
                 (1997)
Allinson H   Hollingbourne the history of a Kentish
                 parish (2002)
Allinson H   Life in the workhouse the story of the
                 Milton Union (2005)
Armstrong   The economy of Kent 1640-1914 (1995)
Arnold R   The Furthest Promised Land, English
                 Villagers, New Zealand Emigrants of the
                 1870s (1981)
Baines D   Migration in a mature economy (1985)
Ball E   Aided immigration from Britain to
                 South Africa 1857-1867 (1991)
Bellingham P   Sittingbourne & Milton (1996)
Carrothers W   Emigration from the British Isles (1929)
Charlwood D   The long farewell settlers under sail
                 (1981)
Cresswell A   The Swing riots in Kent (2003)
Hobsbawn E   Captain Swing
& Rude G
Hook D & R   Boxley the story of an English parish
Ambrose   (1999)
Horn P   Joseph Arch, The Farmworkers' Leader
                 (1971)
Johnson S C   A history of emigration from the United
                 Kingdom to North America 1763-1912
                 (1913 reprinted 1966)

Johnston H J	British emigration policy 1815-30: 'shovelling out paupers' (1972)
Kitson J	The British to the Antipodes (1972)
Kohli M	The golden bridge - young immigrants to Canada 1833-1939 (2003)
Lansberry F	Government & politics in Kent 1640-1914 (2001)
Melling E	The Poor (Kentish Sources IV) (1964)
Melrose K	Luddenham & Stone by Faversham (1993)
Murdoch A	British emigration 1603-1914 (2004)
Poor Law Commissioners	Annual reports
Shepperson W	British emigration to North America (1957)
Simmons A	Old England, New Zealand (1879)
Stevens J	Faversham's reluctant exiles (1996)
Winnifrith J A	History of Appledore (1973)
Woodcock G	A social history of Canada (1988)
Wright C	Kent through the years (1975)
Yates N, Hume R, & Hastings P	Religion & society in Kent 1640-1914 (1994)

Pamphlets

Allinson H	Alfred Simmons friend of the farm worker (1989)
Lord Brabazon	State Directed Colonisation its Necessity in the 19th Century (1886)
Evans E	Hollingbourne and the Duppa family (1995)
Hopker D	Money or blood (1988)
Iota	The Labour Dispute in Kent (1878)
Jebb J	A sermon preached in the parish

church of East Farleigh on occasion of emigration of eight families from that parish to Australia (1838)

Simmons A   State Directed Colonisation, The Proposal Explained and Defended (1886)

Simmons A   Words of Warning to Agricultural Labourers and Other Working Men (1885)

Articles & Theses

Archaeologia Cantiana volumes as cited

Arnold R   Cantium winter 1974 : A Kentish exodus of 1879

Bygone Kent articles by Michael Weller as cited

Carlton F   A Substantial and Sterling Friend to the Labouring Man - the Kent and Sussex Labourers' Union, 1872-1895; Unpublished M.Phil. thesis, 1977, University of Sussex

King D J Francis   From the Weald to Wellington - A history of six pauper families who emigrated from Staplehurst in Kent to Port Nicholson in Wellington, arriving in April 1840; Unpublished thesis diploma in local history, 1991, University of Kent

Power P   The Home Visitor and District Companion Vol XII, 1885

Simmons A   Evidence to Royal Commission on Agriculture, 1881

Records of Unions & Parishes searched

<u>Union records</u>

Some minutes of each of the following unions were studied either at the centre for Kentish Studies, Canterbury Cathedral Archives:

East Ashford, West Ashford, Blean, Bridge, Canterbury, Cranbrook, Dartford, Faversham, Hollingbourne, Maidstone, Malling

<u>Parish records</u>

Some records of each of these parishes were studied at the Centre for Kentish Studies or Canterbury Cathedral Archives:

Aldington, Aylesford, Bearsted, Benenden, Biddenden, Borden, Boughton Monchelsea, Boxley, Brenchley, Brenzett, Burmarsh, Charing, Chart Sutton, Chevening, Cranbrook, East Malling, Egerton, Fairfield, Goudhurst, Headcorn, High Halden, Hucking, Leeds, Linton, Marden, Mersham, Nettlestead, Queenborough, Pluckley, Sandhurst, Sellindge, Staplehurst, Stockbury, Stowting, Warehorne, Wateringbury, West Peckham, Westwell, Yalding

Index

Growing up in Edwardian London –

Maude's Memories

Now published for the first time, this is an unusual and charming book; a first hand account of growing up in Edwardian London.

In 1962, when she was 70, Maude Barker wrote down memories of her early life for her grandchildren.

The daily life of a comfortable working-class family in Brixton and Peckham is brought to life. The lively streets ringing with the cries of costermongers, organ-grinders and muffin men. Visits to the Crystal Palace and the seaside are described with relish. The flourishing dress-making business which Maude's sisters carried on from home is vividly described. The effect of the First World War on the lives of ordinary Londoners is shown.

The growing independence of women is reflected in Maude's experiences of working as a typist in the City.

All is enhanced by the sketches Maude made.

SYNJON BOOKS

ISBN 978 0 904373 11 0

www.synjonbooks.co.uk

Shadrach Blundell

His Family & Property, 1580 to Modern Times

The family history of the Blundells of East Bergholt, Suffolk, Horley, Surrey, Deptford, Greenwich and Chelsfield, Kent and their disputed estates.

Based on many years of careful research, the topics covered include:

- Rumours of riches
- Overcoming the loss of great estates
- Chancery squabbles over 100 years
- Australian Pioneers, Convicts & Immigrants
- Barnado's Child Exports to Australia

SYNJON BOOKS

ISBN 0 904 373 07 X

www.synjonbooks.co.uk

A London Life,
1930-1960:
Other Days, Other Ways

The author's vividly realised recollections of her South-East London childhood during the 1930's are a delight. Brought up by loving parents, her mother a Quaker of strong, idealistic principles and her father a quiet, convinced Communist, she also had the cheerful and practical care of her aunt.

Just when the new interests of grammar school beckoned in the forties, the war brought air raids and evacuation. When Dorothea returned home, the family was bombed out and removed to a house on Bromley Common.

Living in rural Bromley then seemed heavenly, though it proved little safer from enemy action. In the fifties came work, marriage and babies and at last a move to suburban Bromley.

This is a charming account of life in the south-east of London at New cross, Brockley and Bromley in a period of great change.

SYNJON BOOKS

ISBN 0 904 373 10 X

www.synjonbooks.co.uk

'Where Duty Calls Me'

Napoleonic War Experiences of Rifleman William Green

A new expanded edtion detailing his campaigns in northern Europe, Spain & Portugal, the recent discovery of his war medal, the ceremony to mark the erection of a memorial stone, and the historical background

"This is a most interesting & unusual book...a jolly good read and highly recommended." Medal News June/July 2008

Index, bibliography, & chronology; 144pages, 9 illustrations; paperback with coloured gloss card cover

SYNJON BOOKS

ISBN 978 0904373 12 7

www.synjonbooks.co.uk